African American Inventors

Lucent Library of Black History

Stephen Currie

LUCENT BOOKS
A part of Gale, Cengage Learning

GALE
CENGAGE Learning

Detroit • New York • San Francisco • New Haven, Conn • Waterville, Maine • London

GALE
CENGAGE Learning™

LIBRARY OF CONGRESS CATALOGING-IN-PUBLICATION DATA

Currie, Stephen, 1960-
  African American inventors / by Stephen Currie.
      p. cm. -- (Lucent Library of black history)
  Includes bibliographical references and index.
  ISBN 978-1-4205-0121-6 (hardcover)
  1. African American inventors--Biography. 2. Inventions--United
States--History. I. Title.
  T39.C865 2010
  500.89'96073--dc22
                                                            2009038456

Lucent Books
27500 Drake Rd.
Farmington Hills, MI 48331

ISBN-13: 978-1-4205-0121-6
ISBN-10: 1-4205-0121-6

Printed in the United States of America
  2 3 4 5 6 7 14 13 12 11 10

Printed by Bang Printing, Brainerd, MN, 2nd Ptg., 08/2010

Contents

Foreword

It has been more than 500 years since Africans were first brought to the New World in shackles, and over 140 years since slavery was formally abolished in the United States. Over 50 years have passed since the fallacy of "separate but equal" was obliterated in the American courts, and some 40 years since the watershed Civil Rights Act of 1965 guaranteed the rights and liberties of all Americans, especially those of color. Over time, these changes have become celebrated landmarks in American history. In the twenty-first century, African American men and women are politicians, judges, diplomats, professors, deans, doctors, artists, athletes, business owners, and home owners. For many, the scars of the past have melted away in the opportunities that have been found in contemporary society. Observers such as Peter N. Kirsanow, who sits on the U.S. Commission of Civil Rights, point to these accomplishments and conclude, "The growing black middle class may be viewed as proof that most of the civil rights battles have been won."

In spite of these legal victories, however, prejudice and inequality have persisted in American society. In 2003, African Americans comprised just 12 percent of the nation's population, yet accounted for 44 percent of its prison inmates and 24 percent of its poor. Racially motivated hate crimes continue to appear on the pages of major newspapers in many American cities. Furthermore, many African Americans still experience either overt or muted racism in their daily lives. A 1996 study undertaken by Professor Nancy Krieger of the Harvard School of Public Health, for example, found that 80 percent of the African American participants reported having experienced racial discrimination in one or more settings, including at work or school, applying for housing and medical care, from the police or in the courts, and on the street or in a public setting.

It is for these reasons that many believe the struggle for racial equality and justice is far from over. These episodes of discrimination threaten to shatter the illusion that America has completely overcome its racist past, causing many black Americans to become increasingly frustrated and confused. Scholar and writer Ellis Cose has described this splintered state in the following way: "I have done everything I was supposed to do. I have stayed out of trouble with the law, gone to the right schools, and worked myself nearly to death. What more do they want? Why in God's name won't they accept me as a full human being?" For Cose and others, the struggle for equality and justice has yet to be fully achieved.

In many subtle yet important ways the traumatic experiences of slavery and segregation continue to inform the way race is discussed and experienced in the twenty-first century. Indeed, it is possible that America will always grapple with the fallout from its distressing past. Ulric Haynes, dean of the Hofstra University School of Business has said, "Perhaps race will always matter, given the historical circumstances under which we came to this country." But studying this past and understanding how it contributes to present-day dialogues about race and history in America is a critical component of contemporary education. To this end, the Lucent Library of Black History offers a thorough look at the experiences that have shaped the black community and the American people as a whole. Annotated bibliographies provide readers with ideas for further research, while fully documented primary and secondary source quotations enhance the text. Each book in the series explores a different episode of black history; together they provide students with a wealth of information as well as launching points for further study and discussion.

Introduction

African Americans and Invention

If asked to think of a famous inventor, most Americans would probably name technological geniuses such as Thomas Alva Edison, best known for his pioneering work with light bulbs and electricity, or the Wright brothers, Wilbur and Orville, who built the first airplane that could fly under its own power. Aside from these men and a few others, though, inventors are relatively anonymous. Although the typical American can easily rattle off the names of half a dozen cable television stations, for example, few people today know who created the first working television. The same can be said for the inventors of everyday goods such as Velcro, breakfast cereals, and laptop computers.

In some ways the lack of focus on inventors is perfectly reasonable. The inventor matters a good deal less than the invention itself. American drivers think about cars quite often, for example, but their thoughts tend toward questions of how they can afford their monthly payments, how many more miles they can drive before they need to stop for gas, and whether they ought to have a mechanic figure out where that whining sound is coming from. They seldom wonder where early machinists and engineers got the idea for the car in the first place—or who those early automotive pioneers were. For many modern-day

Americans, then, stories of imaginative inventors and their creations take a figurative back seat to more important issues.

The obscurity of inventors, however, is in some ways unfortunate. Most of the things people use and rely on every day, from computer modems to reflective road signs and from canned foods to toaster ovens, were made possible by the insight and hard work of one or more inventors. Quite often the stories of these men and women are compelling. Some of these tales tell of people such as Edison, who spent weeks, months, or even years of their lives creating machines to solve one vexing problem after another. Others tell of important discoveries made almost by accident. Some are about highly educated men and women who used technical training to create new inventions. Still others are about gifted amateurs who learned what they needed to know as they went along.

Each inventor, moreover, reflects the world he or she lived in. By studying inventors and their work, it is possible to learn a great deal about the past—and about the present as well. In the early days of the United States, for example, some of the most important inventions were designed to make farming easier and more productive. Later on, inventions focused on heavy machinery, and later still, on electricity. Recently, computer-related devices and space-age technology have made up a large percentage of American inventions. Through the lens of invention, it is easy to see how the United States moved over time from a heavily agricultural nation to an industrial economy and finally to a high-tech knowledge-based society.

African Americans

The connections between inventors and the wider world is perhaps particularly true in the case of African Americans. The lives and achievements of African American inventors over time not only show the advance of technological progress; they also function as snapshots showing how blacks were typically viewed in American society. The earliest black inventors were ignored or scorned by white Americans, who refused to admit that African Americans could match whites in science and technology—or in any other field, for that matter. Later on, white Americans began to accept that *some* blacks might show unusual talent and mechanical abilities, but argued that these innovators were hardly

An exhibit at the George Washington Carver Interpretive Museum displays influential African American inventors that serve as a focus of pride for black Americans.

representative of the race as a whole. Only recently have African American inventors been accepted as something other than curiosities. These perceptions neatly reflect the prevailing white attitudes toward blacks during the same time periods.

Similarly, the stories of African American inventors also speak to the way that blacks have perceived themselves and how they have functioned as a community through time. It is fair to say that many black inventors could not have accomplished what they did without the support—emotional and financial alike—of other African Americans. As the years have gone by, black inventors have increasingly drawn on this support and acknowledged the debt they owe both in words and in actions. In addition, African American inventors have typically served as a focus of pride for American blacks. Like African American writers, physicians, and athletes, they are examples of what black Americans can accomplish, even in the face of prejudice and hostility. In this way black inventors have encouraged and helped to unify ordinary African Americans.

The stories of black American inventors are stories about science, technology, and individual discoveries, of course. African American scientist George Washington Carver became famous for the hundreds of inventions he created out of peanuts and sweet potatoes, for example, and any discussion of Carver acknowledges his brilliance, his utter dedication to his work, and his contributions to science. The same is true of other black inventors, from electrical expert Lewis Latimer to hair care entrepreneur Madam C.J. Walker and beyond. Without exception, these tales

The Patent System

———————————◼———————————

Just as authors and composers can copyright their books and music, inventors can often patent their inventions. In the United States, patents are issued by the federal government. They are often used to determine who was the first person to invent a particular device or procedure; more important, they give inventors the sole legal right to manufacture or to profit from their inventions. Currently, patent rights extend for twenty years. During that time it is illegal for anyone else to produce or market the invention—or something extremely similar—without the patent holder's permission. Those who do can be taken to court. In the terminology of the legal system, they are infringing on the inventor's patent.

Not all inventors apply for patents, however. Getting a patent can be a difficult and expensive process. The patent office charges fees for applications, and inventors who are seeking patents often must hire artists to make detailed drawings of their creations or attorneys to advise them on legal matters. Even the simplest patent application, moreover, requires inventors to fill out forms and keep track of the process. The patent system thus favors the well off and the well educated. Inventors without much money, inventors without the know-how to complete the forms, and inventors who are only dimly aware that a patent office even exists—all of these may never manage to patent their inventions. Over time, many African American inventors, in particular, have not obtained patents for their work.

of discovery are intriguing. Technologically speaking, they help explain how the world came to be the way it is, and in more human terms, they provide insight into how inventors work, think, and dream.

But the stories of African American inventors go further. While they are certainly about science and discovery, they are also about what it means to be African American in a white-dominated society. The story of Carver, for example, is not simply the story of one man's determination to find new uses for crops, nor even the tale of a scholar pushing back the boundaries of science. Carver's story also reveals the difficulties faced by a black man in a world filled with prejudice, and it speaks to the desire of gifted African Americans to help the less fortunate among them. Similarly, though the story of Walker is in part about hair care, it is just as much about the pride African American women took in the success of one of their own. And the life of Latimer reveals—and to some degree, caused—subtle changes in the way white Americans viewed blacks. The stories of black inventors, then, are not just stories about people, but stories about *a* people. At their most fundamental, they are stories about what it means—and what it has meant—to be black in the United States.

Chapter One

Early Black Inventors

People of African descent have lived in what is now the United States almost since the beginning of European settlement. The lives of the earliest African Americans, however, were very different from the lives of their European counterparts. Europeans who came to America during the 1600s and 1700s did so largely by choice; Africans, in contrast, were pulled from their homes and families against their will. Once in North America, Europeans were generally free, but the majority of African Americans were slaves. Between the mid-1600s and the end of the Civil War in 1865, most American blacks were someone's property. They could be forced to work whenever their owners required it, and they could be beaten or even tortured for any reason at all. In 1860, just before the Civil War began, about 4 million African American men, women, and children were enslaved.

To be sure, not all pre–Civil War blacks were slaves. In 1860, for example, the free African American population numbered in the hundred thousands. But though free blacks had more control over their lives than slaves had over theirs, being a free African American was far from easy. State and colonial governments usually drew sharp legal distinctions between blacks and

Between the 1600s and the end of the Civil War, most African Americans were viewed as property, like this group of slaves owned by Kentucky planter James Hopkinson.

whites. They often denied African Americans the vote, access to education, and other rights that whites usually took for granted. Moreover, practically all white Americans before the Civil War believed that blacks, as a race, were intellectually and morally inferior to whites. "In casting the eye over the world we find, here and there, large masses of human beings of African origin," notes Indiana minister and politician James Mitchell, who, though an opponent of slavery, spoke for many. "But we find little in these masses that is of an elevated character."[1]

Invention and African Americans

Given these circumstances, inventing was extremely difficult for African Americans of the pre–Civil War period. Slaves typically spent their days engaged in exhausting, repetitive farmwork that left little time or energy for the experimenting and tinkering that inventions usually require. Most slaves were uneducated, moreover, and knew little of the outside world. Slaves were not permitted to patent inventions, and even if they were, they would probably not have been allowed to profit from them. And the strong racial prejudices of the time meant that even free blacks usually lacked the education, the time, and the resources to be inventors.

But although inventing was difficult, it was not impossible. This was partly because of the relatively undeveloped technology at the time. While a scientific background was certainly useful for an inventor even then, the world of the early 1800s was a simple place, technologically speaking, and the inventions of the period were simple as well. Developing a more efficient farm tool, say, did not usually require a well-equipped laboratory or a degree in physics. It simply called for a keen mind and an intimate familiarity with farmwork. Nothing prevented African Americans, even slaves, from creating inventions such as these, and in fact many blacks did exactly that.

For African Americans, inventing could also be a road to some success. It was easy enough for whites to ignore most examples

Though credited to white farmer Cyrus McCormick, the mechanical reaper was created in part by McCormick's slave Jo Anderson.

of blacks' ingenuity and intelligence. The average white American had no particular need to read the writings of black authors, for example, or to purchase goods from an African merchant. New inventions, however, were different. A good invention could improve people's lives, reduce their workload, or increase their wealth. Thus, a white person who refused to use or buy an invention simply because it was created by a man or woman of African heritage was behaving foolishly. By building a new machine or coming up with a clever new way of doing something, a free African American might make money. And slave or free, a black inventor might even achieve some respect from whites, however grudging.

James Forten

Born in Philadelphia in 1766, James Forten was one of the best-known blacks of the early 1800s. An antislavery activist, a leader of Philadelphia's African American community, and a highly successful businessman, Forten earned the respect of blacks and whites alike. Apprenticed to a sailmaker at a young age, Forten made his money by running a sailmaking factory; by some estimates he earned well over $100,000 from this business.

In addition to his business sense and his work against slavery, Forten is also remembered as an inventor. Many books on African American inventors assert that Forten developed and patented a device that made sails easier to operate. Although most sources are vague about the details of the invention, including the year it was created, a few of these sources attribute the bulk of Forten's earnings to this invention.

But while Forten may indeed have tried to improve sail technology, it seems doubtful that he invented anything that was truly new. "There is nothing to substantiate this [idea]," writes Forten's biographer, Julie Winch, pointing out that no patent was ever issued to Forten or to any of his associates. If any such invention existed, moreover, it almost certainly was neither revolutionary nor especially lucrative. Unless further information is found, then, Forten is probably more accurately remembered as a remarkable businessman and a committed leader of his people—but not as an inventor.

Julie Winch, *A Gentleman of Color*. New York: Oxford University Press, 2002, p. 73.

It can be difficult, however, to determine which inventions during this period were actually created by blacks. That is particularly true for slaves, who could not apply for patents to lay legal claim to their inventions. Nothing prevented a slaveowner from passing off a slave's discovery as his or her own, then, and it is extremely likely that many masters did exactly that. And while free blacks were certainly better off than slaves, they did not enjoy many legal protections either. It is easy to imagine a white inventor of the time stealing the ideas of a free African American, believing that the court system would never side with a black person. As a result, at least some inventions patented by whites before the Civil War may well have been the creations of black inventors instead.

Some evidence supports this possibility. In particular, several historians believe that one of the great inventions of the early 1800s might have been created at least in part by a black man. The mechanical reaper, a harvester that picks crops when they are fully mature, was patented in 1834 by a white Virginia farmer named Cyrus McCormick. But though McCormick held the patent for the reaper, his slave Jo (or Joe) Anderson was involved in the project as well. Today, it is not clear what role Anderson played in making McCormick's invention a reality. While the best evidence suggests that Anderson's main function was simply to assist McCormick—as one writer points out, Anderson "is not recorded as claiming any significant role"[2] in the project—some historians believe that Anderson suggested ideas to McCormick, and a few historians speculate that the driving force behind the development of the reaper was not McCormick, but Anderson.

Benjamin Montgomery

While no one knows how much impact Jo Anderson had on the invention of the reaper, historians have documented several unequivocal cases of slaves inventing something new and important. One of the most famous of these slaves was a man named Benjamin Montgomery. Born in Virginia in 1819, Montgomery was owned for many years by Joseph Davis, whose brother Jefferson later became the president of the Confederacy. As a young adult, Montgomery was unusually capable and intelligent, and Joseph Davis responded by giving Montgomery opportunities that were not available to the average slave. Montgomery proved particularly strong at surveying and mechanics; Davis once wrote that Montgomery had "few Superiors as a Machinist."[3]

In the late 1850s, now living and working on one of Davis's plantations in Mississippi, Montgomery took on a practical problem. Steamboats often traveled the rivers near Davis's land. The water in these rivers, however, was often quite shallow, and the boats' rotating propellers sometimes snagged on the river bottom. To solve the problem, Montgomery drew up a plan for a propeller that was slanted slightly. The slant kept the propeller securely in the water and made the boat steadier as well. "The blades cut into the water at an angle," writes a historian, "causing less resistance and therefore less loss of power and jarring of the boat."[4] Montgomery soon built a working model of the propeller and attached it to a steamboat. It had exactly the effect he wanted.

Montgomery was the most famous slave known to have been an inventor, but he was not the only one. In the early 1800s a Massachusetts slave known as Ebar devised a new way to make brooms. Ned, a slave on a Mississippi plantation, developed a cotton scraper in the 1850s. (Ned's master was quite willing to credit his slave for the invention, but tried to patent the device himself on the grounds that whatever a slave created was legally the property of the slave's owner. Government officials, though, denied the request.) A North Carolina slave named Stephen Slade came up with an innovative way to dry tobacco leaves so they turned a bright yellow, which appealed to buyers and raised the prices his owner could charge. And a number of other slaves are mentioned in historical records as inventors, mainly of farm tools and household objects.

The Temple Toggle

Men like Montgomery and Slade notwithstanding, though, free blacks made up the largest group of African Americans known to be inventors prior to the Civil War. One of the most important of these inventors was a free man named Lewis Temple. Born in Virginia in 1800, Temple moved as a young adult to New Bedford, Massachusetts. New Bedford was a major seaport, which was known at the time as an important center for the whaling industry. Because whale oil, or melted blubber, was much prized as

The toggling harpoon invented by Lewis Temple improved upon the traditional single-pointed design and helped increase whalers' catches.

a source of fuel, ships routinely set out from New Bedford to troll the oceans in search of whales. If a ship caught enough whales, its owners and crew could all make excellent money.

Capturing a whale, though, was difficult and dangerous. First, the crew had to maneuver close enough to the whale to strike it with a harpoon—a sharp-tipped spear with a long rope attached to the handle. Unfortunately for the sailors, the harpoons of the 1820s and 1830s were not reliable. While the sharp tips went easily enough into the flesh of the whales, they often fell out again once the injured and irritated whales started thrashing around in the water—and after the harpoon strike, most whales did exactly that. If the harpoon fell out, the whale usually swam to safety. The ineffective tips of the harpoons were costing sailors money and making their jobs more difficult. As one historian put it, by the early 1840s "the urgent need of a new and better instrument [was becoming] daily apparent."[5]

Temple was not a whaler himself, but he was an experienced blacksmith. In the mid-1840s, Temple took on the challenge of building a better harpoon. After experimenting with various models, he created a spear with not one point but two. In Temple's design, both points were intended to penetrate the whale's flesh. By means of a device called a toggle, however, the first point to strike the whale would turn at a right angle after piercing the whale's body, locking the harpoon in place. This design added strength to the harpoon and made it much less likely to fall out. In addition, the toggling harpoon typically slid further into the whale than the single-pointed harpoons that preceded it. Where earlier harpoons caught onto the whale's skin and blubber, Temple's invention was designed to fasten itself to the muscle—a design that also kept the harpoon in place.

Temple never patented his invention, and it is not clear how much money—if any—he received for his ingenuity. He did receive plenty of credit for his work, however. Even without a patent, the invention quickly became known as the "Temple toggle." Whalers who used the new double-pointed harpoon saw that Temple's device dramatically increased their catch, and word spread throughout New Bedford and other whaling ports. Before long, whalers everywhere were using Temple's design. As one early-twentieth-century researcher concluded, "It is safe to say that the Temple toggle was the most important single invention in the whole history of whaling."[6]

Other Inventors

Prior to the Civil War, a number of other free blacks also made names for themselves as inventors. In 1821, for example, Thomas Jennings of New York received what may have been the first patent granted to a black American; his patent was issued for a new method of dry cleaning clothes. A decade or so later, Henry Blair of Maryland patented a tool for planting seeds. George Peake of Ohio was another early black inventor; though he apparently held no patents, he developed a new type of mill that sped up the process of grinding grain into flour without heavy machinery. Peake was not an entirely admirable character. In his youth he not only deserted from his army regiment but took most of his regiment's payroll when he left. Still, his hard work and ingenuity helped make him a "highly respected citizen"[7] among both whites and blacks in his home near Cleveland.

Another Ohioan, Henry Boyd of Cincinnati, invented a new design for bed frames around 1830. Boyd's design used a wooden rail to connect the bed's headboard and footboard, making the bed much sturdier than most competing models. The bed was also unusual in that it used no iron bolts. Boyd was proud of his design and lost no time trying to market it. "This newly invented Bedstead," he wrote in a newspaper advertisement, "is warranted to be superior to any other ever offered in the West."[8]

Boyd's bed was an impressive achievement, particularly given the inventor's background. Born in Kentucky, Boyd had spent his first eighteen years as a slave before purchasing his freedom and moving to Ohio around 1820. Cincinnati was free territory, but the people of the city were not welcoming, and no one was willing to give him a job. As an early account of his life puts it, "Day

After purchasing his freedom, Henry Boyd invented a sturdier design for bedframes which led him to open his own factory.

after day did Henry Boyd offer his services from shop to shop, but [just] as often was he repelled [that is, sent away], generally with insult, and once *kicked*."[9] Still, Boyd persevered, eventually finding work as a carpenter. After creating his bed design, he left his job to open his own factory.

Even then, hostility toward Boyd remained. His factory was destroyed by fire at least twice; the fires were probably set by racist whites in an attempt to force him out of business. Nor did Boyd ever patent his design. A few sources suggest that government officials told Boyd that patents were not available to Afri-

Benjamin Banneker

Benjamin Banneker, an African American who lived from 1731 to 1806, was one of the most remarkable men of his time. Though he was not technically an inventor, he had many of the characteristics of one—an inquiring mind, a passion for science, and an enthusiasm for machinery. His interest in astronomy led him to create an annual almanac each year, for which he calculated the times of sunsets, the phases of the moon, and other astronomical events. After analyzing the mechanism of a watch, he built what was probably the first clock ever constructed in the British North American colonies. He was an able architect, too, who was deeply involved in the planning and building of Washington, D.C.

Banneker, a free black from Maryland, was aware that whites of his time held a very low opinion of African Americans. He recognized that his abilities made him extremely unusual among the blacks of his day, most of whom were uneducated and enslaved. Rather than attributing his success to native talent, though, Banneker believed he was an example of what virtually any African American could achieve if given the opportunity. He spent much of his life trying to change people's minds on this subject, and to an extent he succeeded. As Thomas Jefferson put it, Banneker was strong evidence that the lack of achievement by African Americans "is merely the effect of their degraded condition and not proceeding from any difference in the stature of the parts on which intellect depends."

Quoted in John S. Butler, *Entrepreneurship and Self-Help Among Black Americans.* Albany: State University of New York, 1991, p. 58.

can Americans. Boyd's design was eventually patented by another Cincinnati cabinetmaker, a white man named George Porter. Though there is no clear proof, historians speculate that Porter acted as Boyd's agent, applying for the patent on Boyd's behalf to ensure that competitors could not copy the original design.

If Porter's patent was indeed designed to protect Boyd's invention, however, the scheme was unsuccessful. Other furniture makers, recognizing the cleverness of Boyd's design, ignored Porter's patent and quickly manufactured beds based on the same principle. Most of these beds were inferior, Boyd believed, but it was difficult for customers to distinguish Boyd's own products from those of other manufacturers. "Caution," Boyd warned shoppers in another ad for his product. "There are imitations of this Bedstead [on the] market very much resembling it."[10] In the end, Boyd took to stamping his name on his products so people could identify the genuine article. Even today, his beds are highly prized. In 2006, for instance, a Boyd original bed frame in less than perfect condition sold for more than $6,000.

Norbert Rillieux

The free black inventors in the years before the Civil War had much in common. Most were born in the North or in the northernmost tier of slave states, notably Maryland, Virginia, and Kentucky. Few had much formal education; some were illiterate. Most knew little of the world beyond the eastern United States. But that description did not apply to all early African American inventors. In particular, it did not apply to the most famous and successful black inventor of the time—a Louisiana scientist named Norbert Rillieux.

Born in 1806, Rillieux grew up in and around the city of New Orleans. His father was a white man from France with a background in engineering. His mother was a former slave with three European grandparents and one grandparent of African descent. According to Louisiana law, however, that one grandparent was enough to categorize her as black, and the same logic applied to young Norbert. "The prevailing legal definition of the period," write authors Michael W. Markowitz and Delores D. Jones-Brown, "was that 'one drop' of African blood made a person 'negro' or 'colored.'"[11] Thus, though seven of his eight great-grandparents were as white as anyone in New Orleans, the African origin of Rillieux's other great-grandparent meant that, legally speaking, the state viewed Rillieux as black, too.

By American standards, New Orleans was a cosmopolitan place with a thriving free black community. Still, even in New Orleans racial prejudice was common. Hoping to shield him from racism and give him a better education as well, Rillieux's parents elected to send their son to school in France. He proved to be a deeply thoughtful student and a hard worker. Upon finishing school, he was hired to teach mechanics and engineering in Paris. He also pursued an interest of his own by doing research on the steam engine, a relatively new invention at the time.

Rillieux's work with the power of steam soon convinced him that steam engines could be used in the processing of sugar, a major crop in his home state of Louisiana. Many farmers in the area planted sugar cane, an important source of sugar, but turning these plants into usable sugar required several complicated steps. The last of these steps was particularly dangerous and difficult. It called for evaporating the water from a sugary solution so only the sugar would remain. In the early 1830s, this step was accomplished through a procedure known as the "Jamaica Train," in which workers poured the hot solution back and forth between enormous kettles until the water was gone. Rillieux suspected that he could use steam as the basis for a new and improved system of evaporating the water.

The Double Evaporator

In 1833 Rillieux returned to New Orleans to work on the problem. His first ideas were not successful, but Rillieux persisted. Before long he put together a model for a device that he called a "double evaporator." In this design, the steam produced by the heated sugar solution was recycled to raise the heat of the solution even further. Though Rillieux's initial model showed promise, he did not have enough money to create a working evaporator. After several unsuccessful years of trying to convince wealthy business leaders to support him, he managed to get funding from a Louisiana planter named Theodore Packwood. Packwood's money allowed Rillieux to buy the equipment and materials he needed to complete the project. In 1843, after years

Rillieux spent the majority of his childhood in the New Orleans area. The picture shows the city as it might have looked when Rillieux was a boy.

of hard work, Rillieux patented the sugar industry's first double evaporator.

As with Lewis Temple's toggle harpoon, it was immediately clear that Rillieux's invention was a huge improvement over what had come before. The double evaporator saved time, cut costs, and produced a higher quality sugar. By capturing and recycling the steam, moreover, it kept the steam away from workers and shielded them from the risk of burns. Sugar planters clamored for Rillieux's machine. With production costs suddenly lower, sugar became less expensive and more readily available to the average American. The benefits for Rillieux were perhaps even greater. As the patent holder, Rillieux received a share of the proceeds from every evaporator sold in the United States. His earnings quickly rose to a point that few African Americans of the time could match.

Still, Rillieux's money did not bring him happiness. During the 1840s and 1850s, as the Civil War approached, the white majority in New Orleans became more and more hostile to African Americans. State and city leaders passed new laws that restricted the movements of blacks and harassed them in other ways. In the mid-1850s, for example, free blacks were forced to carry passes to prove that they were not slaves. Accustomed to the freedoms of France and the relatively tolerant New Orleans of the past, Rillieux was deeply offended by measures such as these. Moreover, although Rillieux continued to make money from his evaporator, he believed that many white American scientists and academics ignored him and his achievements simply because of his race. This treatment made him increasingly angry.

In the late 1850s, Rillieux turned his back on his native land. He emigrated to France, where he remained for the rest of his life. By most accounts, Rillieux received better treatment in France than he had in America. He still did not achieve the recognition he deserved, however. Many French scientists were reluctant to admit that Rillieux's evaporator worked as well as it did. Their attitude infuriated and saddened Rillieux. When he died in 1894, a friend attributed his death not to his advanced age—he was nearly ninety—but to Rillieux's distress over the lack of respect he had experienced through so much of his life.

Though Rillieux's background distinguished him from other African American inventors of his time, in the end he was no better able than any other to escape the stigma of his race. Whether slave or free, educated or illiterate, trained scientist or gifted amateur, the fundamental truth for black inventors of the period was the same. However clever their designs, however remarkable their work, they were African Americans first and inventors second. Rillieux's financial success could not buy him the respect he craved in a racist society. Temple's redesigned harpoon lined the pockets of the white men who ran the whaling industry, but did not increase his own wealth. And despite Montgomery's remarkable mechanical knowledge, he remained enslaved until the Civil War brought slavery to an end.

Still, the lives of these early inventors demonstrated that African Americans could be as creative as anyone. Despite the hardships they faced, men like Rillieux, Boyd, and Montgomery developed

Eli Whitney and the Cotton Gin

Cyrus McCormick's reaper was one of two revolutionary new farming machines developed and patented in the early years of the United States. The other was the cotton gin, a device which separates the fibers of the cotton plant from the seeds. This machine was patented in 1794 by a white man, Connecticut native Eli Whitney. Like McCormick's reaper, Whitney's machine automated a process that previously had been done by hand, saving time and energy and allowing farmers to produce a much larger crop. No one doubts Whitney's ingenuity in developing this machine, but as with McCormick's reaper, African American slaves may deserve some of the credit as well.

It is known that Whitney visited several cotton plantations in Georgia before building his machine. Most historians agree, too, that slaves on many plantations used crude handmade separators of their own devising. Several observers believe that Whitney saw one or more of these devices in action during his visits and adapted the basic principles into the machine that made him famous. "Slaves made certain appliances experimenting with the separation of the seed from cotton," wrote Henry E. Baker, a patent examiner in the early 1900s who had a particular interest in the inventions of African Americans, "which, when observed by Eli Whitney, were assembled by him as the cotton gin." As with the reaper, the facts of the story will probably never be known.

Quoted in Patricia Carter Sluby, *The Inventive Spirit of African Americans: Patented Ingenuity*. Santa Barbara, CA: Greenwood, 2004, p. 13.

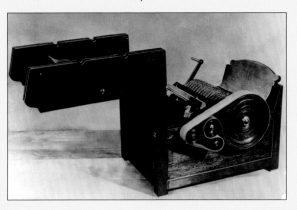

Though the cotton gin was credited to a white man, Eli Whitney, some suggest African American slaves deserve some credit for the device.

useful and important inventions that improved the lives of blacks and whites across America and beyond. They stood as counter-examples to the prevailing notion that African Americans were in every way inferior to whites. Though they could not erase the prejudice most white Americans felt toward blacks, their inventions at the very least challenged these assumptions. And by challenging American attitudes, they paved the way for greater acceptance of black inventors and inventions in the future.

Chapter Two

Mechanics and Tinkerers

Economically speaking, the United States in the later 1800s was a country in transition. In the early part of the century, the United States had been a heavily rural society with few large factories and very little mechanized transport. By 1880, though, life was changing considerably. Cities were growing ever larger. Agriculture, though still vital, was yielding its primary position to manufacturing. Sailing ships were giving way to steamboats, horse-drawn carriages to trains. In the period after the Civil War, in particular, every year seemed to bring more factories, bigger cities, new railroad tracks, and improved manufacturing methods. The United States was becoming a very different place.

The period of rapid economic change that followed the Civil War is often known as the Industrial Revolution. The Industrial Revolution was made possible by several factors, including a steady influx of immigrant laborers and improved access to coal, iron, and other raw materials. The Industrial Revolution was also sparked, however, by a growing spirit of invention across the United States. Americans, both black and white, experimented endlessly with new ideas and machinery during this era. Between the end of the Civil War and 1900, Americans patented well over 600,000 different inventions. Indeed, as historians Allan Nevins and Henry Steele Commager assert, "Americans probably patented more numerous and more ingenious inventions [during these years] than any other people."[12]

The best-known American inventors of the Industrial Revolution were white. Alexander Graham Bell, for example, is widely remembered for his work developing the telephone, which he patented in 1876. Thomas Edison earned his first of many patents in 1869. But African American inventors played a vital, if less obvious, role in creating the new industrial society, too. Enthusiastic tinkerers and expert mechanics who were fascinated by technology, these black inventors devised machines and processes that added to the nation's economic strength. Without their contributions, the Industrial Revolution would have progressed much more slowly than it did.

Working on the Railroad

Black inventors of this period worked with machinery of all kinds. If they had a specialty, though, it was railroads. Many of the most notable African American inventors of the Industrial Revolution created devices that made train travel easier, cheaper, and safer. That was not a coincidence. American railroads hired thousands of black workers, mostly as general laborers. Over time many of these employees became very familiar with the workings of trains. They knew which railroad technologies needed improvement, and the more inventive of them took on the challenge of making these improvements themselves.

And in truth, the railroads of the time were very much in need of improvement. The trains of the mid-1800s were slow, unreliable, and dangerous. That was a problem for all Americans, whether they rode as passengers on trains or not. Effective transportation was critical to the country's continued economic growth. A fast, efficient railroad system would allow companies to speed raw materials to factories for processing—and the finished products to consumers all across the nation. With so much attention paid to railroads during this period, it is no surprise that many inventors—black as well as white—made trains their focus.

Since the railroads employed blacks as general laborers, many African American inventors of the Industrial Revolution created devices that improved train travel.

One of the most successful of these train-related inventions was a direct response to an extremely dangerous part of railroad work: coupling railroad cars, or joining them to form a train. In the 1870s and 1880s this process was done manually. The front and the back of each train car had a coupler, a hitch with a hole. To put two cars together, workers would back one car toward the other until the front coupler of the rear car met the rear coupler of the car in front. Then a worker would insert a large metal pin into both couplers at once, connecting the cars. Unfortunately, this task required perfect timing. Workers who tried to insert the pin a second too early—or a second too late—risked being crushed between the cars. Many railroad workers lost arms and legs in exactly this way, and some died. As a poem of the time put it,

Suddenly there comes a messenger;
God have mercy hear them pray;
As they hear the fearful story—
Killed while coupling cars today.[13]

The problem could be solved by developing a machine that would join cars automatically, and many inventors tried to do just that. One of these was an African American railroad worker named Andrew Jackson Beard. Born in 1849, Beard worked as an adult at an Alabama railroad yard, where he saw the dangers of coupling cars firsthand. In the 1890s he began working on the problem. After many months he built an automatic coupler that could join railroad cars both quickly and safely. "Horizontal jaws engage each other to connect the cars,"[14] he wrote, explaining the mechanism of his invention. Beard patented the device in 1897 and called it the Jenny Coupler. Seeing an opportunity to manufacture and market Beard's invention, a group of businessmen paid him $50,000—an enormous sum of money at the time—for the rights to his patent.

"The Ingenious Folding-Window Ventilator"

Humphrey H. Reynolds was another African American railroad worker who set out to solve a problem by inventing something new. Reynolds was an employee of the Pullman Company, a large and successful business best known for manufacturing passenger cars for trains. He worked as a porter, which required him to travel frequently aboard the railroads and attend to the needs of the passengers. Unfortunately, train travel at the time was far from comfortable. With the windows shut, the interior of a train car usually grew hot and stuffy. Open windows, on the other hand, typically brought in more dust and smoke than fresh air. It seemed impossible to find a comfortable balance between the two extremes.

Like Andrew Beard, Reynolds had an inquisitive mind. Working on the problem during his spare time, he developed a device that he called a ventilator. The ventilator filtered out the worst of the smoke and grime that poured through the open train windows, allowing passengers to enjoy the benefits of the outside air without choking on it. Reynolds patented his invention in 1883. Soon afterward, the head of the Pullman Company, Reynolds's employer, arranged to have ventilators installed on every car it produced. That brought Reynolds's invention plenty of notice and much approval as well; one news article referred to it as "the ingenious folding-window ventilator in use on all Pullman cars."[15]

The Industrial Revolution in America

The effect of the Industrial Revolution on the United States is easy to see. In 1820 about nine of every ten Americans lived in rural areas, and even people in cities and towns often earned their living making agricultural tools or buying, selling, and shipping farm products. By 1890, in contrast, fully one-third of all Americans lived in cities, and that figure was steadily increasing. More and more of the city dwellers, in addition, worked in manufacturing or had commercial jobs that did not focus on agricultural trade.

The transportation system likewise changed during this time. As late as 1840, the country had less than 3,000 miles (4,800km) of railroad track. Those who wanted to travel long distances boarded ships or made a long and difficult journey overland in stagecoaches or wagons. But the railroad boom was about to supersede these older forms of travel. In 1880, just forty years later, almost 90,000 miles (144,000km) of track ran through the United States.

These changes were not necessarily positive ones. Factories spewed pollutants into the air; trains were dirty and smelly. Factory workers were underpaid and labored long hours, often in intolerable conditions. Many commentators of the time disliked the quick pace of an industrial society and the growing emphasis on material goods. They urged a return to the quieter rhythms of rural life. But the Industrial Revolution, once set in motion, was impossible to derail.

In factories like the one pictured in Pittsburgh, Pennsylvania, workers often labored in intolerable conditions for long hours.

However, the Pullman corporation did not pay Reynolds for the use of his device. Nor did company officials fix the problem when Reynolds pointed out that Pullman was guilty of patent infringement. The corporation's strategy of ignoring Reynolds might have worked for many black inventors. Few African Americans of the time would have dared go up against a wealthy and powerful corporation, no matter how sure they were that they were in the right. Reynolds, however, did not shy away from confrontation, and he successfully asserted his rights to his invention. As a news account put it, "He got out of the service of the Pullmans, sued them, and got a verdict for ten thousand dollars."[16]

Elijah McCoy

Other blacks devised train-related inventions as well, though most did not benefit from these creations financially. In 1890, for example, an inventor named Philip Downing received a patent for an electrical switch. Landrow Bell patented an improvement

Black engineer Elijah McCoy developed an automatic lubricator while shoveling coal for the Michigan Central Railroad. Now abandoned, the Railroad was headquartered here at Michigan Central Station in Detroit.

to train smokestacks in 1871. A.B. Blackburn developed a new type of railroad signal in 1888. Many of these inventions, like the creations of Beard and Reynolds, proved quite useful to the railroad industry—and by extension, to the American economy. But important as these inventions were, none of them improved railroad technology nearly as much as the creations of a black man named Elijah McCoy.

Born in Ontario, Canada, in 1844, McCoy grew up there and in nearby Michigan. He was fascinated by machinery from an early age. As a teenager, he worked in a machine shop; later, he spent several years in Scotland, where he studied mechanical engineering. Around 1865, when the Civil War was coming to a close, McCoy returned to Michigan and began looking for a job as an engineer. But racial bias denied him a position that met his talents. No matter how competent, creative, and intelligent McCoy was—and by all accounts he was all three—the white employers of Michigan were not ready to hire a black man to fill an engineering post.

To make ends meet, McCoy eventually took a job for which he was overqualified: a fireman on the Michigan Central Railroad. A fireman's main duties were shoveling coal into the train's engine, where it was burned for fuel, and oiling the engine to make it run at peak efficiency. Of the two tasks, the second was the more time consuming. Train engines were made up of dozens of parts, most of them made of metal. When the train ran, these pieces rubbed against each other, wearing them down. The constant rubbing also created intense heat, which presented a fire hazard. To make the parts last longer and to reduce the risk of fire, the engine had to be oiled every two hours or so. The oil cooled the engine and coated the parts, protecting them from wear. Unfortunately, the train could not run while the fireman was oiling the engine. As a result, trains rarely ran for more than two hours at a time.

The Drip Cup

McCoy believed he could devise a more efficient method of lubricating engines, one which might eliminate the all-too-frequent oil stops. He thought up possible solutions while he was on the job, and after leaving work for the day he ran experiments to test

The Not-So-Real McCoy

The expression "the real McCoy" is often used to mean "the genuine article." Offered a one-hundred-dollar bill in payment for a few small items, for example, a cashier in a convenience store might wonder whether the bill was a fake—or whether it was "the real McCoy."

Many books that discuss Elijah McCoy's life and work claim that he was the original "McCoy" referred to in the phrase. As the story goes, some of McCoy's inventions were imitated by others, but the imitations were not as good as McCoy's original products. Tired of these fakes, railroad officials began demanding "the real McCoy"—that is, the product manufactured by McCoy himself. The phrase soon moved into popular use, according to this view, and developed the broader meaning it carries today.

However, most experts on word and phrase origins reject this theory. The phrase "the real McKay" was current in Scotland when Elijah McCoy was still a boy, and "the real McCoy" is most likely a variation of this term. Nor do McCoy's inventions seem to have much to do with the popularity of the phrase in the United States. "The real McCoy" appears for the first time in print in 1908, long after McCoy patented his best-known inventions, and no early mentions of the phrase directly refer to Elijah McCoy and his works. It is doubtful, then, that the phrase has any relationship to the great African American inventor.

these ideas in his workshop at home. In the early 1870s, after many wrong turns, he created a system that worked. McCoy's method was based on a so-called "drip cup," a container that held oil and released it into the engine at a steady rate. That made it possible to lubricate the engine automatically. Better yet, the drip cup worked even when the engine was in operation. Thanks to McCoy's automatic lubricator, trains were now able to travel many miles without stopping—speeding rail traffic and saving shippers and customers money.

McCoy took out a patent on his lubricating machine in 1872. The invention, he wrote, "provides for the continuous flow of oil on the gears and other moving parts of a machine in order to keep it lubricated properly and continuously and thereby do away with the necessity of shutting down the machine periodically."[17] Most railroad officials who studied the device saw its value and hurried to install it on their own trains. In an ugly footnote, some changed their minds when they realized that the drip cup was the invention of an African American. Even these officials soon recognized, though, that they could not afford to continue with the old method when McCoy's new discovery was so much more effective. Before long, nearly all American railroads used McCoy's invention or something that worked on similar principles.

McCoy, in turn, continued to invent. Over the next few years he developed several improvements to his original lubricator and patented these as well. Later, he devised drip cups for use in other kinds of engines. By the time he died in 1929, he had taken out patents for inventions of all kinds, from lawn sprinklers to ironing boards, and his career had brought him some minor celebrity even outside the black community. "Elijah McCoy, a Negro inventor," read one newspaper account from 1926, "has taken out fifty-seven patents in the United States and ten in Europe. The universally used lubricating cup for machinery is one of his inventions and later ideas of his are receiving serious consideration in the laboratories of the country."[18]

Jan Ernst Matzeliger

African American inventors made names for themselves in industries other than railroads, too. William A. Lavelette of Washington, D.C., for instance, patented two improvements for printing presses in 1878. One year later Thomas Elkins earned a patent for an early method of refrigeration. Joseph Lee of Massachusetts developed a machine that could automatically reduce loaves of bread to crumbs. Joseph Dickinson, an organ builder by trade, established his own organ factory and held patents on several organ designs.

Perhaps the greatest black inventor of the Industrial Revolution, though, was a man named Jan Ernst Matzeliger. Matzeliger was born in 1852 in Suriname, a Dutch possession on the northern coast of South America. Like McCoy, Matzeliger had an interest in mechanics and an aptitude for it. At the age of ten he became an apprentice in a Suriname machine shop. But Matzeliger also had a desire to see the world. When he was nineteen he joined the crew of a merchant ship. According to some sources, he quickly became the machinery expert on board the ship, called upon to fix anything that went wrong. A year or two later, though, his ship made a stop in Philadelphia, and Matzeliger decided to abandon shipboard life and make a new home in the United States instead.

Matzeliger's time in Philadelphia was brief, however. Like McCoy, he could not find employment that suited him. Race was almost certainly the main issue, as it was with McCoy, but Matzeliger's poor English skills probably played a role, too. Before long he moved to Boston and then to the nearby city of Lynn, Massachusetts, which was known for its production of shoes. For a time he operated a sewing machine in a shoe factory. The work was dull, repetitive, and unsatisfying, but it did put food on the table. To

Matzeliger's Machine

As professor and author Dennis Karwatka writes, Jan Matzeliger's reworked lasting machine made an enormous impression on those who witnessed its first demonstration in 1885.

[The machine's] main working component was a single pincers resembling an ordinary pair of pliers with the jaws thinned and bent. A worker placed an insole and an upper on a last and positioned the last on the machine. The machine drove a tack, turned the shoe, pleated the leather, drove another tack, and continued until the shoe was finished, exactly reproducing the technique used by hand lasters. The job took one minute.

Those who saw it could hardly believe their eyes. Working five times faster than a human laster, the device perfectly lasted seventy-five difficult pairs of women's shoes. Other machines had performed parts of these operations; this was the first to combine so many complex steps and produce shoes indistinguishable from handmade ones. And it could handle all shoe styles and any grade of leather.

Dennis Karwatka, "Against All Odds," americanheritage.com. www.americanheritage.com/articles/magazine/it/1991/3/1991_3_50.shtml.

make himself more employable, Matzeliger studied English and physics at night. Even so, he could not find a better job.

Shoe Manufacturing

Since Matzeliger's job at the shoe factory required little thought, he was free to turn his attention to other things. He soon began analyzing the process by which the shoes were made. Only a generation or so earlier, shoes had been created by professional shoemakers. These were craftsmen who produced one pair of shoes at a time, often made to order for a specific customer. The factory in Lynn did things differently. It used an assembly line system in which shoes would pass through several different work stations. At one station, for example, a worker might cut out soles; at another, workers would sew parts of each shoe together. Most of the workers had machines which helped them do those jobs. In theory at least, this procedure sped up the manufacturing process, making shoes less expensive and more widely available.

There was a problem, however. One important step in shoe manufacture is known as "lasting." This term refers to building the "last"—the upper part of the shoe that encloses the foot—and then attaching it to the sole. In the early 1870s the lasting process was carried out exclusively by human workers. Lasting was delicate work which required a skilled and steady hand. Not only were there no lasting machines, but conventional wisdom held that such a machine could not exist. "No man can build a machine that will last shoes and take away the job of the laster," a laster boasted once, "unless he [can] make a machine that has fingers like a laster—and that's impossible."[19]

The lack of an effective lasting machine slowed the shoe manufacturing process considerably. No matter how quickly the machines could turn out other parts of the shoe, the whole procedure came nearly to a halt when it came time for the lasting to be done. As a result, factories could not supply enough shoes to meet consumer demand. That cut into profits, raised prices, and lowered the income of the other workers in the factory, whose pay was based on the number of shoes the factory produced. As a factory worker himself, Matzeliger recognized the problem. However, he did not share the standard view that the lasting process could never be automated. At some point in the late 1870s, he began to try to construct a lasting machine of his own.

"Seven Pages of Complicated Drawings"

The process was long, difficult, and deeply frustrating. Matzeliger had no money to buy equipment, so he had to build models out of materials that he could obtain for little or no cost. He tried design after design, but several years passed and he seemed to be no closer to success. In 1880, though, Matzeliger's hard work and persistence finally paid off. Using wires, wood, and a cigar box, he put together a crude model of a lasting machine. Though the device could not actually last shoes—a working model would have required much more expensive parts—Matzeliger was certain that his design, once built, would prove effective.

The next step was to try to patent the invention. To do that, Matzeliger had to construct the actual machine, and that meant finding the money to buy the materials he needed. Accordingly, he worked out a deal with two investors. In exchange for money to build a working model of his device, Matzeliger promised to give the investors a share of whatever he earned from its sale. This was not an unusual arrangement for would-be inventors, either in the 1880s or today. While Matzeliger would be sacrificing some of his potential profits, the deal made sense. Without a working model, he could never get a patent, and without a patent, he could not earn anything from the machine at all.

Matzeliger soon completed his model and submitted his design to the patent office. The machine was extremely complex; as one historian puts it, his patent application consisted of "seven pages of complicated drawings and eight pages of printed material specifying how his invention worked."[20] Many sources say that the patent officers were initially unable to figure out the workings of the machine and that Matzeliger had to give them a demonstration before they would issue the patent. At last, in 1883 Matzeliger received the patent he had worked so hard to achieve. Over the next two years he added improvements to make his lasting machine more durable and more effective.

Revolutionizing an Industry

Matzeliger's invention was an immediate success. By removing the bottleneck caused by the lasters, it enabled factories to turn out as many as seven hundred pairs of shoes a day, compared with the previous average of about fifty. In addition, it halved the

Jan Matzeliger's lasting machine revolutionized the shoe manufacturing industry. By replacing human lasters with Matzeliger's machine, daily shoe production greatly increased.

cost of producing a pair of shoes, with most of the savings being passed on to the customer. The only people who were unhappy with Matzeliger's invention were, of course, the lasters. They tried to minimize the damage by arguing that automation only increased the need for skilled laborers. "The machine must be operated by an expert laster," asserted one worker, "otherwise the machine is of no effect. The machine is virtually only an assistant to the laster."[21] But their argument convinced no one. The lasting machine soon came to replace the lasters altogether.

Matzeliger did not live long after completing his machine. In 1886 he became ill with tuberculosis. Three years later, at the age of thirty-seven, he was dead. Despite his untimely death, though, Matzeliger was an important figure in the history of American industry. By creating a machine widely believed to be impossible, he completely changed the way people manufactured shoes. "Not many individual inventors would be able to influence, much less revolutionize, a whole industry,"[22] writes author and historian Portia P. James. Matzeliger, she adds, was one of the few who could—and did.

The African American inventors of the post–Civil War years did not have an easy path. Racism prevented McCoy and Matzeliger from finding work that used their exceptional minds to the fullest—or indeed at all. The Pullman Company tried to ignore Reynolds's ventilator patent. Inventors like Beard spent most of their time laboring at dangerous and unappealing railroad or factory jobs. Nor is there any way of telling how many African Americans of the period had invention ideas stolen from them— or how many might have invented if they had not lacked money, education, or encouragement.

Still, black inventors during the Industrial Revolution fared better than their predecessors. American society after the Civil War prized inventiveness and ingenuity, thereby providing a path to success for blacks who had those traits. Though discrimination was still a major issue, white Americans seemed increasingly willing to judge an invention by what it did rather than by the race of the person who had invented it. And it was certainly easier for the African American mechanics and tinkerers of the 1870s and 1890s to obtain patents than it had been for men like bed maker Henry Boyd just a few decades before. By 1900, then, black inventors were still very far from the mainstream. But the distance was beginning to shrink.

Chapter Three

The Age of Electricity

Of all the new technologies developed during the late 1800s, a few stand out as exceptionally important. The telephone, for example, allowed people to talk to each other from one state or country to another—even across oceans. The light bulb provided reliable illumination for homes, businesses, and city streets. Movies, originally known as "moving pictures," not only gave pleasure to millions of people at the time but led to the development of television and other ground-breaking innovations. All three of these inventions, along with plenty of others, changed the way people looked at the world and how they lived their lives.

Nearly all of the most important inventions of the late nineteenth century have one thing in common, though, and that is electricity. Without electric power, the telephone could never have been a reality, and the light bulb as we know it today would have been only a dream. Nor could movies, automobiles, sound recordings, and other vital inventions of the time have developed as they did without a reliable source of electricity. Indeed, electric power was so central to the discoveries of the time that the period from 1870 into the early 1900s is often called the Age of Electricity.

Thomas Edison, a white man, is generally considered the most important force behind the Age of Electricity. Remembered today especially for his work with electric light, sound recordings, and movies, Edison patented more than one thousand inventions and opened Americans' minds to the possibilities of electric power. But though Edison was the best known of the thinkers who showed how electricity could be used for the public good, he was far from the only one. Among the others were two African American men, Granville T. Woods and Lewis Latimer, men whose keen minds, intellectual curiosity, and thorough understanding of electricity made them central figures during this time as well.

Thomas Alva Edison showed Americans the benefits of electricity.

Electricity

Electricity was not a new discovery in the late 1800s. Even early peoples had known about this type of energy. For centuries, for example, people have been familiar with static electricity—the charge that can be felt when a person rubs a cat's fur, say, and then touches another object. Lightning, another form of electricity, was known to long-ago societies as well. And cultures that caught fish were often familiar with electric eels and other marine creatures that carry an electric charge. But familiarity with these forces did not imply understanding. Indeed, for many centuries people did not know that lightning and static electricity were essentially identical.

During the 1600s and 1700s Western scientists began to study electrical energy in earnest. Through the work of researchers such as Benjamin Franklin, understanding of electricity gradually increased. Franklin and others like him ran important experiments that led scientists to understand the properties of electricity, the relationship between electricity and magnetism, and the way that electricity is used in the nervous system of the human body. Still, few scientists explored whether electrical energy might have practical applications. Well into the 1800s, electricity was viewed more as a scientific oddity than as a force that people might be able to harness and use for themselves.

In the absence of electricity, Americans of the time used a variety of fuels. One common choice for illumination was oil—much of it obtained from the blubber of whales caught by sailors using Lewis Temple's harpoon. Factories were often built beside waterfalls to take advantage of the power generated by moving water. Farmers occasionally used windmills to harness the force of the wind. Perhaps the most popular fuel of the period, though, was natural gas. Natural gas was easy to burn, and it produced a steady, even light suitable for indoor use as well as for streetlamps. To the people of the 1860s, one historian writes, "gas was such a clean, efficient, inexpensive source of lighting that it seemed improbable that any other mode of illumination would, or could, replace the gaslamp."[23]

Still, a few progressive scientists viewed electricity as a potential substitute for gas. In 1802, for example, British scientist Humphrey Davy built a primitive version of an electric light bulb.

Though the bulb had no practical value, Davy's success intrigued other researchers. Over the next several decades a steadily growing number of scientists and technicians worked on the problem of developing a safe and reliable electric light. Though they did not know if electric light could ever be an effective substitute for gas, they were determined to find out. Little by little they made progress, building on each other's work and moving gradually toward the construction of a reliable and efficient electric light.

The breakthrough came in the late 1870s. After many months of research, Edison found a way to build a bulb that gave off plenty of light, lasted for some hours, and was relatively cheap both to buy and to run. The design was not exclusively his; other inventors had come up with some of these ideas long before he began researching electric light, and an English inventor used many of the same design elements in a light bulb of his own invention around the same time. Nonetheless, Edison was the first to put all these ideas together and demonstrate that an effective electric light bulb could be a reality. Though electric light was slow to catch on among the public, it was evident to scientists and inventors across America that a new age was dawning. Electricity, they realized, was the wave of the future.

Lewis Latimer

One of the first Americans to recognize the potential of electricity was a black man named Lewis Latimer. Born in Massachusetts in 1848, Latimer served in the U.S. Navy during the Civil War. When the war was over, Latimer returned to Massachusetts and got a job with a law firm that specialized in patents and inventions. At first he worked as an office boy, delivering messages and doing other simple tasks that involved little responsibility. Assignments like these made some sense, given his youth and relative inexperience. It is also likely, however, that Latimer's race kept him from being considered for positions that carried more authority—and a larger paycheck.

Latimer did not wish to remain an office assistant for long, though. He soon became intrigued by the work of the company's draftsmen. To apply for a patent, inventors had to provide careful pictures that showed every detail of their inventions. Because most inventors did not have the skill to execute these pictures

Lewis Latimer, Poet

Lewis Latimer was an unusually well-rounded man. In addition to his remarkable scientific abilities, he was a fine musician, a volunteer teacher of English to immigrants, and a poet. Late in his life, he published a small book of his poems. Many of the poems in the book were love poems; others were Latimer's musings on life, death, and the world around him. The following poem appeared in the book he published.

> What is there, in this world, besides your loves
> To keep us here?
> Ambition's course is paved with hopes deferred,
> With doubt and fear.
> Wealth brings no joy,
> And brazen-throated fame,
> Leaves us at last
> Nought but an empty urn
> Oh soul, receive the truth
> E're heaven sends thy recall
> Nought here deserves one thought but love,
> For love is all.

Quoted in Charles R. Brooks, "Black Inventor Helped Develop Telephone, Electric Lighting," *The News* (Frederick, MD), February 10, 1971, p. 10.

on their own, patent lawyers typically had expert draftsmen on staff to create the diagrams. Latimer resolved to learn everything he could about drafting. He studied drawing techniques at home and practiced them whenever he could. Before long, his bosses recognized his talent and promoted him to the post of draftsman. By 1875 he was the head draftsman for the firm. As a later newspaper report put it, Latimer had been "thrust upward by his singular talent and drive."[24]

Latimer's drawing work brought him into contact with many inventors. The most famous of these was Alexander Graham Bell, best known as the inventor of the telephone. Latimer made several drawings which helped Bell claim the patents he sought. To

African American scientist Lewis Latimer believed that electricity could help Americans in new and important ways.

draw these designs as accurately as possible, it was necessary for Latimer to learn as much as he could about Bell's work. In the process Latimer became interested in the principles of electricity, principles which underlay much of what Bell was doing. As Latimer read more and more about electric power, he became convinced that this form of energy could help Americans in new and important ways.

Patents

In the late 1870s Latimer began looking for a job that would allow him time to pursue his new interests in technology. He was eventually offered a position at a company called the United States Electric Lighting Corporation. The head of the company, Hiram Maxim, was already well known among scientists for his work with electric power. Though Thomas Edison had already patented the first truly effective electric light bulb, Maxim believed he could improve on Edison's design. In particular, Maxim thought he could increase the life span of the bulb. Toward that end, he hired the most intelligent and hard-working people he could find—including Latimer.

Latimer spent his first few months in Maxim's employ trying to improve the bulb's filament—the wirelike assembly inside the bulb that gives off the actual light. In 1881, just a year after joining Maxim's firm, Latimer and a colleague patented a new and more efficient way of making filaments, using what their application

Women and Patents

◼

Hard as it was for African American men to patent inventions during the 1800s, earning a patent was considerably more difficult for a woman. Not only were nineteenth-century women usually encouraged to stay out of public life, but women were thought to lack the understanding of science and technology necessary to be inventors. Many sources say that no African American woman received a patent until 1928, when Marjorie Joyner patented a permanent wave machine to curl or straighten hair.

This claim is almost certainly not true, however. In 1884 a woman named Judy W. Reed patented a kneader and roller for bread dough. A year later Sarah E. Goode was issued a patent for what she called a "Cabinet Bed," which combined a bed and a writing desk in one piece of furniture. Though little is known about either Reed or Goode, many historians believe that Reed was African American, and nearly all accept that Goode was black. The first African American woman to patent an invention, then, was most likely one of these two.

called "a continuous strip of carbon secured to metallic wires."[25] The new procedure resulted in better, cheaper light bulbs even than Edison had been able to produce. In the next months Latimer went on to patent several more inventions, each of which made light bulbs longer lasting and easier to manufacture—and each of which brought more money to the corporation. Maxim's confidence in Latimer had paid off.

Latimer did not spend all his time inventing. His work had made him an authority on electric lighting, and Maxim consequently gave him more and more responsibility. Maxim sent him to Philadelphia and other U.S. cities to oversee factory operations. Later, Latimer traveled to England to set up a new factory and to Montreal, Canada, to guide workers in installing electric lights in train stations. In Montreal he even learned some French to communicate with employees who spoke little or no English. "This was my mighty lesson," he wrote years later. "My day was spent climbing telegraph poles and locating arc lamps on them with the assistance of my laborers who seemed much impressed with my effort to speak their native language."[26]

Becoming an Expert

Latimer's boss, Maxim, was a successful businessman and was by all accounts a fine scientist. Nonetheless, he was not well respected by others in his field. "I did not like Maxim and was distrustful of him," an acquaintance said in an 1880 interview. "Several times he had the effrontery to claim to others before my face ideas given him by me."[27] After only a few years of working with Maxim, Latimer apparently could no longer stomach his employer's morals, and he left Maxim's company. In 1884, after a period of unemployment, he was offered a new job as a draftsman—this time with Maxim's greatest rival, Thomas Edison.

In the next dozen years, Latimer held a number of posts with Edison's Electric Light Company (known today as General Electric). One of his main tasks was to work with the firm's legal department. In the growing and increasingly lucrative world of electric light, inventors and manufacturers regularly filed suit against each other for patent infringement. Latimer helped Edison defend his patents against lawsuits from other inventors who claimed he had stolen their ideas; similarly, he assisted in filing suit against

Latimer held a number of posts at the Edison Electric Light Company.

those who unfairly made use of Edison's work. That required Latimer to make a thorough study of each electric device in question, to the point where Latimer's knowledge of electric light surpassed that of almost anyone else alive. Indeed, in 1890 Latimer wrote a book called *Incandescent Electric Lighting,* which for many years was the definitive word on the subject.

In 1896, by now well known and well respected within the industry, Latimer moved on to a new position. Two of the biggest electric companies in the United States had established a special governing body to resolve patent disputes out of the court system, and Latimer was chosen to serve as chief draftsman for this group. Fifteen years later Latimer left this post too and became an independent patent consultant. During these years he also patented several new devices, among them a new type of safety elevator and a mechanism to cool and disinfect air. When he died in 1928, he was mourned as a fine colleague and a brilliant inventor. As an industry group put it, referencing the vital role Latimer had played in the development of electric lighting, "We rejoice in the pleasant memory of having been associated with him in a great accomplishment for all peoples."[28]

Granville T. Woods

Like Latimer, Granville T. Woods was an African American inventor with a particular interest in electricity and electrical devices. Like Latimer, too, Woods was born shortly before the Civil War. Like Latimer, Woods's life was connected to the life and work of Thomas Edison—indeed, Woods was often nicknamed "the black Edison." And again like Latimer, Woods made a career for himself despite little formal education and the realities of racism in late-nineteenth-century America. Despite the similarities, though, Woods's story and Latimer's story had important differences as well.

Not much is known about Woods's early life. Most sources say that Woods was born in Columbus, Ohio, in 1856, but the best available evidence suggests that he was actually born in Australia and came to the United States as a child. As a teenager, Woods seems to have held a variety of jobs, perhaps including stints as a laborer in a steel mill, a railroad worker, and a crew member aboard a steamship. Woods's passion, however, was electrical engineering. Woods read voluminously on the subject, but like many other black inventors, he had difficulty finding work that matched his skills. In 1884, after years of frustration, Woods changed course. Since he could not find an employer who would give him work he wanted to do, he went into business for himself instead. Opening a workshop in Cincinnati, he immediately set out to invent.

Going into business for himself was a wise move in many ways, for Woods was an exceptionally innovative inventor. He was versatile too. Where Latimer's inventions were almost all in the field of electric lighting, and Elijah McCoy mainly focused on engines and oiling systems, Woods developed a wide range of devices. One of his first patents, for example, was for improvements to a steam engine, and perhaps his most important invention was an air brake to improve the stopping ability of trains. His patents also included an egg incubator capable of hatching hundreds, even thousands, of eggs at a time.

African American inventor Granville T. Woods's expertise was in electricity.

Before the Third Rail

Several years before the "third rail" came into general use as a way to propel trains with electricity, Granville Woods patented a different method that relied on similar principles. In 1893 the *New York Times* published a brief article about his invention under the headline "May Drive Out the Trolley: Successful Experiment with an Underground System of Electric Propulsion."

> There was a very interesting and remarkable test to-day on the short section of railroad here [in Coney Island, New York], where the system of underground conduits for electric propulsion invented by Granville T. Woods, the colored electrician of Brooklyn and Cincinnati, is being experimented with. The system consists of a conduit [a long channel or tube], in which are placed at regular intervals hermetically-sealed and watertight boxes, from which project contact points at each side of the slot. These contact points form a connection with a long shoe which is fastened on the bottom of the [train] car and runs in the slot.

> The experiment demonstrated that the device could work even in bad weather. In the reporter's estimation, Woods's invention was a clear improvement over the overhead wires that powered trolleys, which were common at the time. Other observers agreed. "The day of the trolley is past," the reporter quoted an electrician as saying. "I would rather own this patent than any other for electric street-car propulsion in the world."

Quoted in "May Drive Out the Trolley," *New York Times*, September 16, 1893, p. 4.

Still, Woods had an area of particular expertise, and that was electricity. Within a few months of founding his new company, Woods patented a new kind of transmitter for telephones. The following year he invented a device that he called a "telegraphony." This invention combined two of the nineteenth century's greatest innovations in communication—the telephone and the telegraph. The telegraph, invented before the Civil War, allowed messages to be sent through wires using a system of long and short electrical impulses, with different combinations of impulses standing for different letters. Woods's innovation was to add telephone technology to the telegraph system, allowing senders to choose either their voices or standard telegraph codes to convey their messages.

In 1887 Woods perfected an even more important invention. For years, telegraph wires had been a common feature alongside railroad tracks. These wires carried messages to and from stationmasters at various stops along the route. However, it was not possible to telegraph a message between a station and a moving train—or, for that matter, between two moving trains. That created dangerous situations when tracks were washed out or unexpected obstacles lay ahead, and several inventors had tried to build devices that would permit trains to communicate while they were in transit. None had done so, however, until Woods came along.

Woods's device, known by the impressive name of Synchronous Multiplex Railway Telegraph, allowed trains to tap into the telegraph wires along the tracks as they sped along so they could send and receive messages too. "A circuit of wire extends along the track," Woods wrote, describing this device, "and another circuit is carried by the [train] car."[29] It was now possible for engineers and stationmasters to send messages back and forth even while a train was underway. Woods had helped make rail travel safer.

More Inventions

Woods followed this invention with a slew of others, including a safety circuit to cut down on electrical fires and a grooved wheel to increase the electrical current sent to streetcars. Woods is also known today as the inventor of the so-called "third rail," though in truth he shares this distinction with several other thinkers who came up with similar concepts around the same time. The third rail is a method of supplying electricity to trains without using overhead power lines. Instead, workers build a new rail, which carries a powerful electric current and runs parallel to the existing track. Trains are then connected to the rail, giving them all the energy they need. The third rail is a feature of many commuter train lines today.

But although Woods was undeniably a brilliant inventor, he had chronic money problems. "I have been depending entirely upon daily labor [that is, handyman jobs] and what money I could borrow,"[30] he mourned in 1885, five years after starting his business. Woods eventually sold several of his patents to large corporations; the Bell Telephone Company purchased one of his telephone transmitters, for example. The payments he received seem to have been relatively small, though, and Woods had difficulty making money on the patents he kept. Certainly Woods was never wealthy or even well off.

Woods was also forced to defend himself against lawsuits brought by rivals who believed he had stolen their ideas. Although Woods typically had fewer resources than the men who were suing him, he was usually able to fend off their challenges. Twice, Thomas Edison took Woods to court, claiming that Woods had infringed on one of his patents. Both times, Woods won the case. After the second time, recognizing Woods's skills and inventiveness, Edison offered Woods a job in his engineering

Granville Woods helped developed the "third rail," which supplied electricity to trains via electrical boxes along the rail.

department—a job which Woods turned down, preferring to stay in business for himself. Even when Woods won a case, however, he could not celebrate his victory. Defending himself against the suits still cost him both money and time.

Respect and Doubt

Granville Woods died in 1910. Though he had failed to make much money, he had made lasting contributions to technology. Just as Latimer's work with electric lights helped make the Age of Electricity a reality, so too did Woods's improvements to telegraphs, telephones, and trains. Both inventors received plenty of recognition from other African Americans, and each drew the attention of whites as well. One white journalist referred to Woods as "the greatest electrician in the world,"[31] and another said that Woods was "equal, if not superior, to any inventor in the country,"[32] regardless of race. The *New York Times* printed a brief obituary when Latimer died, an honor the paper's editors had not seen fit to give previous African American inventors. And white business leaders showed great respect for Latimer, both as an inventor and as a person, when they asked for his help in resolving patent disputes.

Still, white Americans did not view Woods or Latimer as in any way typical of blacks. Historian Rayvon Fouche argues that Latimer achieved success largely by downplaying his race. "Several times he was asked to speak out on racial issues and each time he said no," Fouche points out. "He was a conservative black man. It would have been hard for him to maintain his economic status and also be outspoken."[33] Woods was also perceived as having a number of "white" characteristics, which in the eyes of the white majority set him apart from most African Americans of his time. "[Woods] is fluent in conversation," one white magazine reporter wrote approvingly, "and his speech is entirely free from dialect."[34] Whites found it easier to categorize Woods and Latimer as exceptions—examples of what blacks could be at their very best, but hardly representative of the African American people.

The accomplishments of Woods and Latimer were both important and impressive. Both men overcame prejudice and poverty, both men persisted in the face of hardship, and both men added enormously to the world's understanding of electricity and its uses. But though Americans in general gave them more attention and respect than most earlier African American inventors had received, Latimer and Woods did not earn much money from their inventions—and their work brought them less fame than they surely deserved. The United States, evidently, was not yet ready to make black inventors either truly rich or truly famous. That would have to wait for another time.

Chapter Four

Moving Forward

The early 1900s were a difficult time for African Americans. Throughout the South and in much of the North as well, racial prejudice spread unchecked. Blacks lagged behind whites in every measure of social and economic progress: They were poorer, less well educated, and more likely to live in substandard housing. Still, despite the problems, there were signs of advancement, and one had to do with invention. During this period, for the first time, African American inventors were able to use their discoveries to become wealthy or famous—or in some cases both. Of previous black inventors, very few had approached this level of success. And the respect received by earlier inventors such as Norbert Rillieux had been grudging at best.

The new ability to earn fame and fortune was partly due to changes in the way whites perceived African Americans. Earlier black inventors had demonstrated to all but the most racist whites that blacks could be inventive and resourceful. Granville Woods, wrote one white journalist, proved "beyond doubt the possibility of a colored man inventing as well as one of any other race."[35] But in truth, the successes of this new wave of inventors had much more to do with the support of other African Americans. Most of these inventors did not try especially hard to move into the white world. Instead, they spent their lives primarily among other African Americans, who often formed the best market for the inventors' work, and who typically provided less tangible help as well. The inventors of this era, then, succeeded mainly because of changes in the way that African Americans were coming to view themselves.

Madam Walker

Of all the inventors of the era, the one with the most compelling story might be Sarah Breedlove Walker, known to millions of her contemporaries simply as "Madam" Walker. Madam Walker's life is particularly intriguing for several reasons. For one, Walker was not merely black, but a woman. Given the sexist attitudes of the day—attitudes as prevalent among blacks as among whites—Walker faced prejudice on two counts. Moreover, nothing in Walker's background and early life suggested that she would climb higher than the typical poor and uneducated black woman of her time and place. That she *did* climb higher, then, is a powerful testimony to her hard work and perseverance.

Sarah Breedlove was born in 1867 to impoverished former slaves who lived in Louisiana. Her early years were difficult indeed. Orphaned before she was seven, she married at fourteen to escape an abusive brother-in-law. By her early twenties, she was a widow with a young child to support. Needing to make a living by any means possible, Walker found work washing other people's clothes and sheets—a long and strenuous task in the days before automatic washers and dryers. For the next fifteen years or so, the only major change in her life was a move from the rural South to St. Louis, Missouri, a city with greater economic opportunities and a thriving black culture. But racism and sexism were prevalent in St. Louis, too, and by 1890, when Walker was in her early thirties, she found it difficult to imagine that she would ever have a better life.

Then Walker's problems grew worse. In the mid-1890s her hair began to fall out, leaving bald spots across her scalp. Though the loss of hair was annoying and embarrassing, it was not unusual for African American women of the time. Poor nutrition was one cause of the problem. Stress was another. The most important factor, however, was the way African American women treated their hair. The American beauty ideal of the time called for women to have long, straight hair. This look was easy enough

Inventor Sarah Breedlove Walker, also known as "Madam" Walker, faced prejudice for both her race and gender.

for many Caucasian women, but most black women had hair that was naturally short and curly. They could achieve the ideal only by twisting, tying, and pulling their hair. Over time, the twists and pulls stressed the hair and the scalp. Hair loss was one inevitable result of this treatment.

With the problem so widespread, enterprising chemists and marketers had developed lotions, powders, and oils designed to stop the loss of hair. These remedies were easy to find in heavily African American sections of St. Louis and other cities. When Walker tried these concoctions, however, she was not impressed. Some of these oils and lotions contained ingredients that caused unpleasant side effects. Others stressed the hair and scalp even further, causing more damage. Few seemed to have any value at all.

Dreams and Hard Work

Since these formulas had not stopped her hair loss, Walker resolved to try to concoct a medication herself. She combined a variety of ingredients in dozens of different ways, always hopeful that each formula would fix her scalp problems. But again

By developing her own line of hair products, Walker was able to achieve millionaire status.

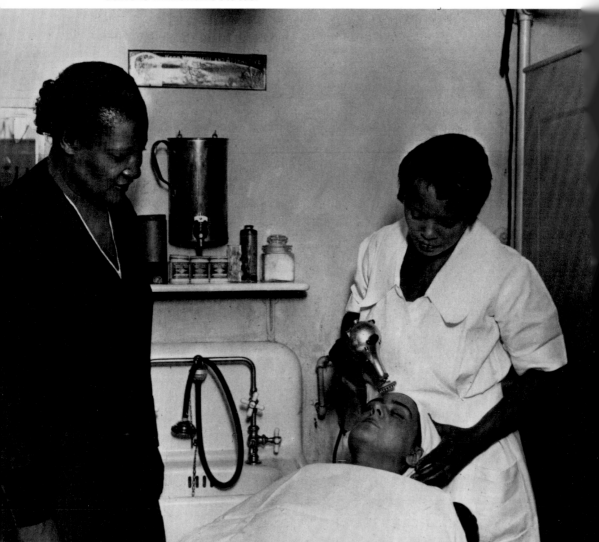

and again, her mixes proved ineffective. Around 1900, however, Walker had a breakthrough. As Walker told the story, she had a visionary dream after a particularly frustrating day of experiments. "A big Black man appeared to me and told me what to mix up for my hair," Walker explained. "Some of the remedy was grown in Africa, but I sent for it, mixed it, put it on my scalp, and in a few weeks my hair was coming in faster than it had ever fallen out."[36]

Whether the result of a dream or the product of hours of tinkering and experimentation, the new concoction did wonders for Walker's hair. Delighted, Walker shared her invention with her friends. The results were promising, and Walker soon developed two other hair care products as well. In 1905 she moved to Denver, Colorado, and began going door to door marketing her inventions directly to black women. At each house she demonstrated her shampoos and oils on potential customers at no charge. Walker was confident that her product would help the majority of these women. And once they had experienced what Walker had to offer, she believed, they would be willing and eager to pay for more.

Walker's gamble was successful. Word of her products spread quickly through Denver and beyond. With help from friends and family members, Walker opened a mail-order business. Then she began making tours of the rural South, winning over new customers by product demonstrations just as she had in Denver. She advertised extensively as well, touting the effectiveness and efficiency of her goods. "Your hair will respond immediately," one ad promised. "In one treatment it will be straight and fluffy."[37] Walker also established a network of African American women who sold Walker's products and split the proceeds with her, helping many of them move toward the middle class.

By 1908 the name "Madam C. J. Walker," which appeared on nearly all of the company's products (C.J. Walker was her third husband, whom she divorced in 1913), was familiar to blacks across the country—and to many whites as well. As more and more customers tried Walker's remedies, sales soared. Before long, Walker was a millionaire—the first African American woman to achieve that status on her own. "I am a woman who came from the cotton fields of the South," she said in a speech once,

Marjorie Joyner

When Madam Walker died in 1919, her successors hired an African American beautician named Marjorie Joyner to run Walker's cosmetology schools. Joyner followed in Walker's footsteps as an inventor. In 1926 she devised an invention that she called a Permanent Waving Machine. This machine consisted of a set of sixteen metal rods, which were suspended from a circular hanger. The rods were placed in and around the customer's hair and then heated. The heat acted to curl hair that was already straight and to straighten hair that was naturally curled. Joyner earned a patent on her invention in 1928.

In addition to being an inventor and an administrator, Joyner was also deeply involved in community and political issues. In 1935, for example, she became one of the founding members of an advocacy organization called the National Council of Negro Women, and she was a strong voice on behalf of blacks in her home city of Chicago. Her work brought her into close contact with a succession of famous people, from educator Mary

McLeod Bethune to former first lady and activist Eleanor Roosevelt and from Chicago mayors Richard J. Daley and Harold Washington to singers such as Lena Horne and Billie Holliday. As one reporter put it, Joyner went "practically everywhere and met practically everyone." She died in 1994 at the age of ninety-eight, active in her community until the end of her life.

Adam Linder, "You Know, I'm 95 and I Know What I'm Talking About," *Chicago Reader*, September 10, 1992. www.chicagoreader.com/chicago/you-know-im-95-and-i-know-what-im-talking-about/Content?oid=880420.

Inventor Marjorie Joyner was also involved in many political and community issues.

detailing her remarkable rise. "From there I was promoted to the washtub. . . . And from there I promoted myself into the business of manufacturing hair goods and preparations. . . . I have built my own factory on my own ground."[38]

Walker spent freely on luxuries. She also devoted much of her fortune, however, to helping the people that had made her rich. Till the end of her life in 1919, she worked hard to educate young African Americans and help them achieve economic self-sufficiency. As an Indiana newspaper put it in 1918, "It is safe to say there is no one belonging to the colored race that is doing more for the education of boys and girls or is helping more struggling young men and women than Madam Walker."[39] Walker's creativity and inventiveness had lifted her out of poverty—and helped do the same for countless other blacks of her time.

Garrett Morgan

Walker's rise from obscurity to dramatic success was paralleled by another black inventor—a man named Garrett Morgan. In some ways, indeed, Morgan's story is similar to Walker's. Born in Kentucky in 1877, Morgan, like Walker, was the child of former slaves. Like Walker, too, Morgan had little formal education and was forced to leave home at an early age to try to make his way in the world. Where Walker made a name for herself through hair care products, though, Morgan's interest lay in machinery. At age fourteen he found work as a handyman in Cincinnati, Ohio. A few years later he journeyed north to Cleveland, where he got a job repairing sewing machines.

Morgan's job provided him with stability and a steady paycheck. It gave him no opportunity to advance, however, and Morgan—again like Walker—was ambitious. In 1907, after much deliberation, he left his job and opened his own business fixing and selling sewing machines. Soon he expanded into tailoring as well. By 1912 he had several dozen employees. With his business flourishing, he devoted more and more of his time to tinkering with machinery and devising and building new inventions. An exceptionally creative man, he impressed others with the breadth and sophistication of his ideas. "He had all these things in his head that just had to come out,"[40] his granddaughter recalled years later.

Morgan's first important invention was a gas mask, which Morgan called a "safety hood." He built the earliest working model of the mask in 1912 and patented it two years later. Intended for firefighters and other emergency personnel, the hood filtered dangerous particles from the air, enabling the wearer to inhale fresh oxygen even while surrounded by smoke. A rescue worker who wore the device, Morgan wrote in his patent application, could "enter a house filled with thick suffocating gases" and nevertheless "breathe freely for some time."[41] Morgan noted that the mask could also be useful for chemists and others who worked in situations where the air might be unsafe.

"A Death Hole"

It did not take long for the public to become aware of the mask. In July 1916 a pocket of natural gas exploded in a work tunnel beneath Lake Erie, near Morgan's home in Cleveland. "The tunnel was turned into a death hole in a twinkling,"[42] reported a newspaper in nearby Sandusky, Ohio. Workers close to the tunnel entrance quickly climbed to the surface, but toxic gases and billowing smoke sealed off the escape route for workers on the far side of the explosion. Several men descended into the tunnel, hoping to reach the victims and bring them out. Unfortunately, the fumes and the gases were more deadly than they knew. Once underground, most of the rescuers were also overcome by the suffocating smoke. A few managed to return safely to the surface. The rest, however, were killed.

The situation looked bleak. "Not a vestige of hope remains that any of the prisoners will be brought to the surface alive,"[43] a local reporter wrote gloomily. But someone at the scene of the accident knew that Morgan lived nearby. Officials quickly summoned him to the tunnel, where he donned one of his hoods and gave hoods to three other men, a group that probably included his brother. Breathing filtered air through their masks, the four men made their way into the tunnel.

The first man found by Morgan and his companions was dead. But the second man they found was still alive. As Morgan put it, the rescuers "discovered from groans"[44] that this worker had not yet succumbed to the smoke and gas. The rescuers hurriedly carried him to safety and returned to see if there were others.

The gas mask, developed by Garrett Morgan, filtered toxic gases and pollutants from the air and allowed the wearer to breathe fresh oxygen. The one here is a slightly updated version of Morgan's original.

According to many modern-day retellings of the story, Morgan and his fellow volunteers eventually saved the lives of twenty or more workers and rescuers. Articles written by local newspaper reporters at the time make it clear that these claims are untrue; it is unlikely that Morgan and his crew were able to save more than two men in all. They did, however, recover the bodies of all the dead. Whatever the survival rate, moreover, the men had acted with extreme courage—and Morgan's safety hood had proved remarkably effective.

Wealth and Respect

Following the episode under Lake Erie, fire departments and rescue squads across the country clamored for hoods of their own. Morgan was happy to oblige. Unfortunately, in an echo of the treatment received by McCoy some years earlier, the leaders of some of these organizations canceled their orders when they discovered that Morgan was black. "Apparently," a present-day source notes, "many people would rather face danger and possibly death than rely on a lifesaving device created by a Black man."[45] Aware that race was an issue, Morgan often posed as a Native American when he demonstrated his device. He may also have occasionally hired a white man to pose as the safety hood's actual inventor. Sadly, these tactics were necessary in an era when many whites still refused to see African Americans as equals.

With his earnings from the safety hood and the continued growth of his tailoring and sewing machine business, Morgan was now quite well off. He soon focused his inventive mind on a new problem—the issue of traffic. In the early 1920s, cars were becoming more and more common on the streets of Cleveland and other cities, but the mixture of cars, trolleys, and horse-drawn carriages made conditions increasingly dangerous. Each vehicle moved at its own speed, and safety equipment was lacking. Intersections were particularly unsafe. Unless a patrol officer was stationed at a given crossing, drivers could not tell whether they should keep going or whether they should stop. This uncertainty led to dozens of accidents.

As an enthusiastic automobile driver—or "autoist," as car drivers were often called at the time—Morgan not only saw the problem firsthand but experienced it as well. Resolving to improve the situation, Morgan soon developed an automated traffic signal. His device included rotating signs that instructed drivers to stop, to go forward at regular speed, or to proceed with caution. Though Morgan's invention was not the first traffic signal, it was nevertheless an important step in the development of the modern stoplight. He sold the rights to his device to the General Electric corporation for $40,000, a remarkable sum of money at the time.

By the time he died in 1963, Morgan had accomplished a great deal. Besides being an inventor, he had become a leader within Cleveland's black community. He served as treasurer of an African American men's organization, ran for political office, and helped to found a newspaper. Morgan also won a number of awards for

Morgan's automated traffic signal, which incorporated rotating signs to instruct drivers, aimed to solve the issue of traffic accidents. Through invention, Morgan was one of the first African Americans to gain widespread recognition and financial stability.

his life and work, including honors from a scientific society and a gold medal from the city of Cleveland. Along with Walker, Morgan was one of the first African Americans to earn both widespread recognition and financial security through invention.

George Washington Carver

Unlike Walker and Morgan, George Washington Carver never became wealthy from his inventions. But perhaps more than either of them, Carver earned respect and fame for his creativity. Born into slavery in 1864, just as the Civil War was coming to an end, Carver grew up in rural Missouri. Although he was poor and often sickly, young George nonetheless stood out for his intelligence and drive. "I had an inordinate desire for knowledge,"[46] Carver wrote years later, recalling his childhood, and the adults who knew him as a boy agreed.

Carver was determined to get an education, no matter the difficulties—and the difficulties were many. As a high school student he worked as a cook to pay his expenses and fit studying into his busy schedule when possible. He applied to Highland College in Kansas, but as Carver reported years afterward, "[I] was refused on account of my color."[47] In fact, the situation was more demeaning than Carver let on. Carver applied to Highland by mail and was accepted. When he arrived at the school, though, Highland officials realized that he was black and turned him away. They had never had a black student, they told him, and were not ready to change that policy.

Undeterred, Carver eventually won admission to Simpson College in Iowa. Even at Simpson, where faculty and students welcomed or at least tolerated him, the situation was not ideal. Money, in particular, remained an issue. For an entire month, he reported afterward, "I lived on prayer[,] beef suet[,] and corn meal."[48] But once again Carver persevered, eventually earning not only a college diploma but a master's degree as well.

Carver's great interest was botany, or the study of plants—a subject that had fascinated him for as long as he could recall. "All sorts of vegetation [seemed] to thrive under my touch," he wrote in a brief memoir. "I was styled the plant doctor, and plants from all over the [area] would be brought to me for treatment."[49] Upon getting his master's degree, Carver took a job teaching and

Peanut Butter

Few foods seem as thoroughly American as peanut butter. With or without jelly, peanut butter has been a favorite food for children and adults in the United States for many generations. Because items made from peanuts are so closely associated with George Washington Carver, many people over the years have assumed that peanut butter was Carver's invention. Indeed, quite a few books and Web sites about Carver available today assert that this is the case. The assumption is not correct, however. Peanut butter was known before Carver even arrived at Tuskegee. The best evidence indicates that peanut butter was the brainchild of an unnamed doctor in St. Louis, who developed it around 1890 to provide protein for people who had difficulty chewing meat.

Though Carver did not invent peanut butter, his experiments with peanuts unquestionably helped to popularize the new food, and Carver certainly deserves credit for that. As the following article in an 1897 Pennsylvania newspaper makes clear, many people before Carver's time viewed peanut butter with suspicion, even distaste:

> A new article, known as peanut butter, is said to be on the market. It is made from the oil of the peanut, and has the flavor of the nut. Like all other products of similar kind, the consumers must be educated to accept it. It is not injurious [that is, does not harm people], and is considered beneficial to some, but it will not take the place of butter from cream very soon.

Gettysburg (PA) *Compiler*, "The Farm in General," November 16, 1897, p. 4.

managing the greenhouse at Iowa Agricultural College, now Iowa State University. He soon earned the respect of other scientists by writing and publishing scholarly papers and by discovering two new types of fungus which preyed on crops and other plants.

A New Opportunity

Though Iowa State had welcomed Carver both as a student and as a faculty member, most American colleges at the time were not so progressive. Like the Kansas college that Carver had tried to

African American botanist George Washington Carver (bottom center) taught as head of the agricultural department at Tuskegee Institute.

attend, they barred blacks altogether. As a result, black leaders had established schools of higher learning specifically intended for African Americans. These schools provided young black people with a place to continue their educations after high school. However, they were seriously underfunded. Unable to buy basic supplies, pay their teachers well, or keep their buildings in good repair, all-black colleges could not function at the same level as colleges that were open to whites.

One of the best known of these historically African American schools was Tuskegee Normal and Industrial Institute in Tuskegee, Alabama. Known most often simply as Tuskegee Institute, this school had been founded in 1881 by a black leader named

Booker T. Washington. In 1896, eager to upgrade his school's faculty, Washington invited Carver to head up Tuskegee's agriculture department. "I cannot offer you money, position or fame," Washington admitted. "These things I now ask you to give up." But even if the job did not advance Carver's career, Washington reasoned, Carver might still consider it out of a sense of responsibility to his fellow African Americans. "I offer you," Washington wrote, "the task of bringing a people from degradation, poverty and waste to full manhood."[50]

Washington's words were persuasive. Carver not only accepted the appointment but spent the rest of his career at Tuskegee. As department head, he used his knowledge of soils, crops, and agricultural techniques to assist poor farmers, particularly African Americans in the South. His first success was reducing farmers' dependence on cotton. Though cotton was an important cash crop in the Deep South at the time, it robbed the soil of nutrients if it was planted in the same fields year after year. Each season, then, the land produced less cotton, cutting farmers' already low incomes. Carver taught farmers how to restore nutrients to the earth by planting crops such as peanuts, peas, and sweet potatoes in rotation with cotton.

Innovation

The addition of peanuts and other new crops did help farmers increase their cotton production. In the process, though, the new methods created an oversupply of sweet potatoes, peanuts, and peas. At the time, these foods made up only a small part of most southerners' diets. Rather than let these crops rot in the fields, Carver spent hundreds of hours in his laboratory devising new uses for them. His creativity and his thorough understanding of biology and chemistry helped him turn out one product after another made from these crops. He turned peanuts into such unlikely goods as cheese, ink, linoleum, and soap, for example, and Carver successfully synthesized vinegar, flour, and much more from sweet potatoes as well.

When Carver died in 1943 he left behind a wealth of new farming techniques, new scientific understanding, and—most of all—new products. His research and experimentation resulted in more than three hundred new products from the peanut and over one hundred more from sweet potatoes. Carver's ingenuity extended to other materials as well. At the beginning of World War II, for example, he developed over five hundred shades of dye. This was necessary because the war had cut Americans off from their usual sources of dyes in Europe. He crossbred plants to create hardier crops that would produce more food. He found new uses for cornstalks, created a variety of products from soybeans and cotton, and—as one biographical sketch puts it—became "the first scientist to make synthetic marble from wood shavings."[51]

George Washington Carver received a fully equipped laboratory for food research from Henry Ford. The laboratory allowed Carver to turn an overabundance of pea, peanut, and sweet potato crops into a multitude of useful products.

Booker T. Washington's prediction that Carver would sacrifice money by moving to Tuskegee was accurate. During Carver's lifetime, U.S. law did not permit inventors to patent most items created from plants, and so Carver had no way of maintaining exclusive rights to his creations. It seems clear, too, that Iowa State would have paid him a higher salary than he was able to earn at Tuskegee. Then again, money never seemed important to Carver. According to some sources, Carver rarely accepted raises when Tuskegee offered them, and many accounts of Carver's life suggest that he had to be reminded to cash paychecks. Nonetheless, Washington was right that Carver's move to Alabama did not make him rich.

But Washington was wrong when he said that Carver would also sacrifice the chance for fame if he came to Tuskegee. On the contrary, Carver became one of the most famous and respected scientists of his time. Carmaker Henry Ford befriended him; so did fellow inventor Thomas Edison. Carver spoke on farm policy to the U.S. Congress, was frequently sought out—especially in his later years—by newspaper and magazine reporters, and won any number of important awards and honors. When he died, he was mourned not just in the South but across the nation—not just by blacks but by whites as well. "Nature chose well when she picked this great Negro to carry on her work,"[52] a Nevada newspaper editorialized the day after Carver's death; sentiments like these were common.

Changes in Perception

During the early 1900s, African Americans had difficulty achieving fame or fortune in any field. In education, in politics, and in business, blacks were denied the opportunities that whites typically took for granted. Like other African Americans who longed to succeed, Walker, Morgan, and Carver all experienced poverty and racial discrimination. Yet despite the hardships, all three achieved dramatic success. Much of the success, of course, was due to their own qualities as people and as inventors. Few Americans from any time or of any race could match these three for ingenuity, intelligence, and drive.

But the successes of Walker, Morgan, and Carver had another cause as well. Even in the face of prejudice and hostility

Richard Spikes

———————————■———————————

Garrett Morgan was one of many inventors who helped make the traffic light a reality. He was not the first African American inventor to try to improve traffic safety, however. That honor probably goes to a man named Richard Spikes, whose career as an inventor was long and varied. Between 1906 and 1962, Spikes patented a number of inventions, including a new type of barber chair, a device that could be used to open a milk bottle and then to cover it to keep it fresh, and what he described as a "self-locking rack for billiard cues."

Spikes's most important invention, though, had to do with cars. By modern standards, the cars of the early 1900s were extremely slow; they traveled no faster than a horse and buggy. The lack of speed made it easy for motorists to use hand signals or their voices to alert others when they were about to change direction. As cars became faster, though, a better system became necessary. In 1913 Spikes met the challenge by developing an electrical turn signal, similar to the ones that are standard equipment on cars today. Like Morgan, he was not the only inventor to tackle this problem. But again like Morgan, he was one of the first—and one of the most successful as well.

Quoted in Keith A.P. Sandiford, *A Black Studies Primer: Heroes and Heroines of the African Diaspora.* London: Hansib, 2008, p. 424.

from white Americans, blacks were beginning to establish systems and institutions of their own. By 1900, large numbers of African Americans remained desperately poor—but taken as a group, members of the black community had enough buying power to make a gifted and confident inventor like Walker into a millionaire. By 1900, lack of education was still a pressing concern in the black community—yet educated African Americans were increasingly able to set up scientific labs, publish newspapers aimed at black readers, and raise the level of education at historically black colleges and universities. Black America in the early 1900s was ready to create its own heroes and heroines. It did so in part by recognizing and saluting some of its brightest minds—the African American inventors of the period.

Chapter Five

Into the Future

Much has changed for African Americans since the 1920s and 1930s, let alone the days before the Civil War, and nearly all of that change has been for the better. The standard of living for American blacks has risen sharply during this period, bringing more and more African Americans into the middle class. Far more African Americans today are college graduates than was true in, say, 1940 or even 1965. Where many state and local governments once kept hundreds of thousands of blacks from voting, African Americans today are a much more significant part of the political process. And fields and professions once off limits to nearly all blacks now typically present few if any barriers to modern-day African Americans.

The news is not entirely positive, however. As a group, American blacks continue to be poorer and less well educated than their white counterparts. Compared to whites, African Americans are more likely to attend failing schools, more likely to suffer from chronic diseases, and more likely to be on public assistance programs. And after many years in which the incomes of blacks rose more quickly than the incomes of whites, the economic gap between the races has recently begun to widen again. "Not all children are benefiting equally from the American dream,"[53] says researcher Julia Isaacs. Still, no one can deny that race has been a much less significant obstacle for blacks of the late twentieth century and the early twenty-first century than it was for their grandparents.

That change is well illustrated by the African American inventors of the modern era—those whose discoveries took place largely after 1950 or so. With few exceptions, these inventors have had an easier time reaching acceptance in the wider world than those who preceded them. Where Americans once reacted with surprise, indignation, or disbelief to the news that an invention had been created by an African American, very few people would respond that way today. It is no longer newsworthy for an African American to devise something new. Consequently, more and more blacks have become successful inventors. Their innovations have come in a variety of fields and have helped improve life for people all over the world.

Frederick McKinley Jones

One of the first of these modern African American inventors was a man named Frederick McKinley Jones. Jones was one of the most remarkable inventors of his time—or indeed any other. During his long career as an innovator, Jones developed a variety of new devices, from automatic ticket-taking machines to a new type of portable X-ray machine. The majority of Jones's inventions, however, had to do with refrigeration and cooling. Indeed, Jones's work in this field has been as important as any other inventor's.

Jones's life was every bit as remarkable as his work. Born in the Cincinnati area in 1893, Jones had a sad and difficult childhood. His mother died when he was very young, and his father sent him to an orphanage when he was just eight. As a teenager, Jones left the orphanage and tried to find work. Though he had not attended school past the sixth grade, Jones was deeply interested in mechanics. He soon got a job at a Cincinnati car repair shop and progressed to the position of foreman. In 1912, however, Jones moved to Hallock, Minnesota, where he took a job as chief mechanic for a wealthy resident who owned a fleet of automobiles.

Over the next few years Jones read widely in engineering, electronics, and science, hoping to develop his mechanical knowledge. He also became an enthusiastic automobile racer. His car,

Inventor Frederick McKinley Jones developed many creations that focused on cooling and refrigeration.

which he built largely according to his own design, was exceptionally fast, and he frequently won the races he entered. After a stint in the military during World War I, Jones returned to Minnesota, where he built a transmitter for Hallock's radio station, created snowmobiles out of skis and old car parts, and developed a portable X-ray scanner for the doctors of the community. By the late 1920s, Jones had become the local expert on mechanics and engineering.

Ultraphone and Thermo King

To this point Jones was unknown outside Hallock. That soon changed, though, and the reason was the movie industry. Through the mid-1920s, movies had no recorded sound. When dialogue

Frederick McKinley Jones and businessman Joe Numero partnered to form a new company, Thermo King, with the aim of developing and manufacturing refrigeration units for trucks.

was necessary, directors broke away from the actors and filmed cards printed with the words of the characters. In the late 1920s, however, it became possible to synchronize recorded sound with the action on the screen, and the first "talkies" were born. These movies became very popular among audiences. Theater owners now had to scramble to find equipment that could play these soundtracks—or lose business to theaters that did upgrade.

Shortly before 1930, a worried theater owner in Hallock asked Jones to devise a system that could play movie soundtracks. Though Jones had only scrap metal and other basic materials on hand, he threw himself into the task with enthusiasm. Before long he built a device which not only played sound but improved the quality of the projected images as well. The theater owner spoke to other business leaders about Jones's remarkable invention. Soon word of Jones's achievement spread to Minneapolis, the largest city in the state, and to a businessman named Joe Numero. The owner of a company called Ultraphone Sound Systems, Numero thought Jones would be an outstanding addition to his staff. In 1930 he hired Jones and brought him to Minneapolis.

Over the next few years Jones more than earned his salary. He came up with improvements to existing Ultraphone technologies and developed a few new technologies of his own, each time helping the company earn customers. In 1935, however, his career took an unexpected turn when Numero got into a discussion with a friend who was in the trucking business. The friend lamented the difficulties of keeping food cold while it was being transported. He had recently lost an entire truckload of food to spoilage because ordinary ice had not kept the truck chilly enough in the summer heat. Numero boasted that Jones, with his impressive mechanical abilities, could build something that would solve the problem.

Though Numero certainly recognized Jones's talents, he meant the boast largely as a joke. But when the friend took him seriously, Numero felt forced to ask Jones to take on the problem. Fortunately, Jones was delighted to try. "We ought to be able to fix up something,"[54] he told Numero after thinking about the issue. Despite Jones's limited education, his difficulty obtaining materials, and his lack of experience with heating and cooling, he soon came up with a refrigeration unit that could keep the inside of a truck extremely cold. Jones showed his invention to Numero, who immediately saw the device's potential. Deciding to switch his focus from sound systems to refrigeration, Numero sold Ultraphone to another telecommunications company. Next, Numero and Jones formed a business partnership and founded a new corporation, which they eventually called Thermo King. Their goal was to develop and manufacture Jones's refrigeration units for trucks.

"A Soft-Spoken Negro Engineer"

Thermo King was not an immediate success. "Forget about that talk that the world will beat a path to your door," quipped Numero years later. "They might do it for a mousetrap, but we had to sweat like hell to start this business."[55] Still, after Jones patented his refrigeration unit in 1940, the device slowly became the standard for trucking companies across the United States. The invention allowed truckers to ship perishable food safely even during the hottest weather, making it possible for food produced almost anywhere in the United States to be eaten anywhere else. As one newspaper columnist writes, Jones's invention "eliminated the problem of spoilage [and] revolutionized the eating habits of Americans."[56]

Jones followed this device with similar innovations meant for refrigerating trains and ships, along with an air-conditioning unit meant for hospitals, several improvements on truck refrigeration technology, and many other inventions. In all, he earned more than sixty patents before his death in 1961. Though Jones never received much notice from the general public for his work, other scientists and technicians certainly respected his accomplishments. During World War II, for instance, Jones's cooling units were widely used to keep blood and medicine from spoiling as they were shipped to the front. The military was happy to acknowledge the system's inventor. "We are particularly grateful for the work of Mr. Fred Jones,"[57] an army official wrote in a letter to Numero.

Even those who appreciated Jones's work, though, could not forget that he was black. Journalists who profiled him or mentioned him in their articles almost invariably highlighted his race. One 1951 news article about Jones's achievements, for example,

Medical Innovators

———————◼———————

Charles Drew (1904–1950) was an African American doctor who became well known during the 1930s and 1940s. Much of his work focused on blood transfusions, in which blood products are taken from one person and given to a patient who is very sick or who has suffered physical trauma. While not technically an inventor, Drew was certainly an innovator in his field. He was the first to set up so-called "blood banks" where blood plasma, or the liquid part of the blood, could be stored until needed. These blood banks proved particularly useful during World War II. By keeping the plasma fresh, military doctors could save the lives of soldiers injured in battle, even when there was no time to evacuate them to a regular hospital.

Drew was not the first innovative African American doctor. In 1893 Daniel Hale Williams (1858–1931) became the first physician to successfully perform open-heart surgery, or an operation on the heart itself. This operation was believed impossible before Williams managed to carry it out, but it has since become standard practice for surgeons. Like Drew, Williams may not have been an inventor as we commonly understand the word today. But as with Drew, Williams's work was both pioneering and tremendously helpful to Americans of all races, both then and now.

referred to the "inventive genius of [this] soft-spoken Negro engineer."[58] In this way, the media and the public thus perceived Jones much as they had perceived Morgan, Walker, and other inventors of the previous generation. On the other hand, phrases such as "inventive genius" underscore the shift toward a more modern way of thinking in which race, while important, was no longer the barrier it had been. Jones was evidence that the white world was increasingly willing to give credit where it was due.

Percy Julian

Jones's work with refrigeration made him one of the most important African American inventors of his time. His achievements were matched, however, by Percy Julian, a scientist who earned dozens of patents in the field of chemistry. Born in Alabama in

African American Percy Julian earned multiple patents in the chemistry field.

1899, just a few years after Jones, Julian was an inquisitive child whose parents were determined to get him an education. Though few African American children of that era went to school much beyond sixth grade, Julian completed high school and then went off to DePauw University in Indiana to study science.

Julian's years at DePauw were rocky. The college refused to house him in a dormitory, and his race made it difficult for him to find a place to stay in the surrounding town. A friend eventually helped him find work in a fraternity house, where—as a later newspaper account put it—he "fired the furnace for room and waited tables for board."[59] Academics were a struggle for Julian at first, too. His all-black high school did not cover all the material DePauw expected incoming students to know. Consequently, Julian began as a "sub-freshman," required to take remedial classes for no credit before being enrolled as a regular student. Once Julian made up his missing coursework, however, he excelled. Indeed, when he graduated from DePauw, he was first in his class.

Upon completing college, Julian was eager to continue to graduate school. He hoped to earn a doctorate in chemistry, and his academic record certainly suggested that he could do so. His professors, however, tried to talk him out of pursuing this goal. Most graduate schools, they told him, would not consider accepting a black student. And even if one did, they pointed out, Julian's job prospects would be bleak. Students who earned doctorates typically went on to teach at colleges and universities, but Julian's professors warned him that he would find employment only at all-black schools, where instructors did not need more than a college diploma. Integrated colleges, they said, would never consider him as an instructor. In their eyes, white students would refuse to learn from an African American, no matter how capable a teacher.

Julian paid little attention. After teaching briefly at Fisk University, an all-black school in Tennessee, he discovered that Harvard University in Massachusetts would accept him as a graduate student. Julian's joy was short-lived, though. Harvard officials soon decided that despite Julian's obvious abilities (and despite the fact that George Washington Carver had successfully taught at Iowa State University some years before), they were not prepared to let a black man teach white students. Though Julian did earn a master's degree at Harvard, he was not permitted to enter the doctoral program.

Even then, Julian did not give up. In 1929 he left the United States for Vienna, Austria, where prejudice against blacks was less significant and where the local university was happy to have him as a student. In Vienna Julian did important research into medi-

The Julian Family and DePauw University

Percy Julian went to DePauw University because his father, James Julian Sr., never had the opportunity. As a boy in Alabama, James Julian attended a school run by a religious organization. One of his teachers was from Indiana and was familiar with DePauw. Noting James's intelligence and desire for knowledge, she once remarked with obvious regret that the boy "should have been able to go to DePauw." Only his race kept him away.

Though James never did attend college, the teacher's comment stayed with him throughout his life. Her words helped him push Percy toward DePauw. And though Percy's DePauw experience was not entirely positive, James and his wife then sent their next four children—Mattie, Elizabeth, Irma, and Emerson—to the school as well. All four received their degrees between 1926 and 1938.

The only Julian child who did not graduate from DePauw was James Jr., the youngest in the family. Though he enrolled at DePauw, he soon transferred to the University of Chicago, where he got his bachelor's degree; he later earned a medical degree from Howard University. In 1970, however, when James Jr. was sixty-eight, DePauw officials decided to award him a bachelor's degree to complete the family connection. The year was well chosen: As a newspaper account put it, 1970 marked both "the 100th anniversary of the birth of [James Jr.'s] father and the 50th anniversary of Percy Julian's valedictory graduation in 1920."

Anderson (IN) *Herald*, "DePauw Will Graduate 6th in Family," May 22, 1970, p. 27.

DePauw University was attended by Percy Julian and four of his siblings.

cal chemistry, some of it in conjunction with a European student named Josef Pikl. Two years later, upon receiving his doctoral degree, Julian returned to the United States. In 1932 he accepted a position as a chemistry professor at—of all places—DePauw, where professors had only recently told him that white students would never accept a black instructor. Attitudes were beginning to change.

Physostigmine, Soybeans, and Hormones

While teaching at DePauw, Julian continued his research. Much of his initial work concentrated on a chemical compound called physostigmine. This substance appears naturally in a plant known as the calabar bean. Scientists were aware that physostigmine could help in the treatment of several diseases. These included glaucoma, an eye disease that can lead to blindness, and an immune system disorder called myasthenia gravis. But it was difficult and expensive to extract physostigmine from the calabar bean, so Julian tried to develop ways to synthesize the chemical— that is, to manufacture it in the laboratory. He worked on this problem with Pikl, his fellow student from Vienna, who joined him at DePauw for this project. In 1935 Julian and Pikl successfully created an artificial form of physostigmine and patented the process. Their discovery is used in treatment of glaucoma and other diseases today.

Abandoning academic life a few years later, Julian moved to Chicago to work in private industry. He used proteins derived from soybeans to improve and create a variety of products, from such basic materials as glue and paint to a new kind of foam used to fight fires by World War II soldiers. Before long, Julian had figured out a way to produce artificial human hormones from soybean plants. Like the physostigmine Julian developed in the lab at DePauw, these hormones had important medical uses. Cortisone, one of these hormones, was used in the treatment of rheumatoid arthritis. Others helped cancer patients or reduced the chances of miscarriage in pregnancy. As before, Julian patented many of the processes he developed to create these drugs.

By any standard, Percy Julian was enormously successful. In 1954 he founded his own business, which he sold seven years later to a large pharmaceutical company for more than $2 million.

When he died in 1975, he held more than 130 patents, including some which had directly improved the health of thousands of sick people. Julian was well respected by his fellow scientists—and by others as well. In 1973, for example, Julian became one of the first African Americans to be elected to the National Academy of

Though chemist Percy Julian dealt with a number of racial issues, his career transcended the skin color barrier.

Sciences. Similarly, readers of a Chicago newspaper once voted him "Chicagoan of the Year."

Julian's road to success was not entirely smooth. Racial prejudice was an issue throughout his life. As late as 1950, when Julian moved his family to the Chicago suburb of Oak Park, some white residents set his house on fire and threw dynamite onto his property in an effort to drive him out of the community. Nonetheless, Julian's career, especially in the 1960s and 1970s, transcended skin color in a way that the lives of previous African American inventors had not. "I've heard people remark that Dr. Julian is a credit to his race," wrote a white Chicago journalist with obvious irritation. "I'd like to correct that statement. He's a credit to the HUMAN race!"[60] And a newspaper article about Julian that appeared shortly after his death did not mention Julian's race until the seventh paragraph. In the opening of the piece, the reporter characterized him simply as "an internationally known research chemist."[61]

Other Innovators

Several other generations of African American inventors have followed in the footsteps of Jones and Julian. Otis Boykin, born in 1920, was among the first of these. A generation younger than Percy Julian, Boykin held a variety of patents, mainly for electrical equipment. Some of his patents were for electronic resisters, which prevent too much electricity from flowing into an appliance. He also created a new type of air filter and patented a supposedly burglar-proof cash register. Boykin is best known today, however, for an invention he built to help heart patients. People with irregular heartbeats often are helped by small devices called pacemakers, which send electric signals to even out the rhythms of the heart. While Boykin did not invent the pacemaker, he did develop a control unit that helped to make the pacemaker feasible.

Another black inventor, Meredith Gourdine, was not only a brilliant physicist but a remarkable athlete. Born in 1929, Gourdine won a silver medal in the long jump at the 1952 Olympics. After earning a doctorate in engineering science, he went on to patent more than thirty devices. His inventions included a meth-

Black inventor Meredith Gourdine earned a silver medal at the 1952 Olympics in addition to patents for more than thirty devices.

od of cooling computer chips, a means of converting coal into electricity, and a system for clearing smoke and fog from rooms or airport runways. Gourdine is also of interest because unlike almost every black inventor who preceded him, he had little difficulty getting a top-notch education. Gourdine was offered a scholarship by the University of Michigan, graduated from Cornell University, and earned his doctorate at the California Institute of Technology. Prejudice against African Americans in education was not gone by any means, but Gourdine's story illustrates that the barriers were falling more and more rapidly.

More recent African Americans have continued to invent. For a time, many of these inventors were connected with the

Ninety-Two Black Inventors

George Washington Murray (1853–1926) was an African American from Sumter County, South Carolina. A farmer, teacher, and inventor, Murray held eight patents on various types of farm tools. He is better known today, however, for his political career. Despite laws and customs that limited the right of African Americans to vote, Murray twice won election to the U.S. House of Representatives. He served from 1893 to 1897, and he was the only black member of Congress at this time.

Murray had a strong appreciation for black history as well as a desire to improve the lives of African Americans of his own era, and he worked to highlight the achievements of African Americans both past and present. In one notable instance, he made a speech in Congress urging that the work of African Americans be included in a proposed celebration of southern technology and scientific progress. "The colored people of this country," he said, "want an opportunity to show that . . . they, too, are part and parcel of that great civilization." He ended his speech by reading aloud a list of ninety-two black inventors and their achievements, a list that has provided a starting point for many researchers since then.

Quoted in *Diversity Works!* "Colors of Innovation," Winter 2007, p. 16. www.scribd.com/doc/2523917/Diversity-Works-Magazine-Black-History-Month-2007.

space program in some way. During the 1970s, for instance, a black man named Robert Shurney devised a waste management system for use on Skylab, an orbiting research station. George E. Alcorn, born in 1942, is known for his work with semi-conductors and with space missiles. George Carruthers helped design a camera that could take pictures on a lunar mission; he also built a device that could detect electromagnetic radiation. And NASA scientist Valerie Thomas invented a method of using mirrors to create a three-dimensional illusion of a distant object.

Of course, space is by no means the only area of expertise for modern-day black inventors. Mark Dean, born in 1957, holds several important patents relating to home computers. Eye doctor Patricia Bath pioneered a way to use lasers in eye surgery. Other black inventors have patented creations ranging from the vital (such as improved engines and new chemical processes) to the entertaining (such as the "T-shirt with Removable Sleeves Convertible to a Hat"[62] patented in 2004 by Fonda Evans of Springfield, Illinois). With access to opportunities for blacks increasing and with racism no longer as rampant as it once was, there seems no limit on what African American inventors can achieve, both today and in the future.

At the same time, the fact that invention by African Americans is now commonplace has had an ironic side effect. While recent historians and educators have highlighted the accomplishments of past African American inventors such as Woods, Walker, and McCoy, the black men and women who are the inventors of today are not generally as well known. In the past, the deeply rooted racism of the United States created significant stumbling blocks for nearly every black inventor. The story of early black invention is therefore in part the story of people who overcame serious hardships—hardships caused mainly by an environment they could not control.

In contrast, the racism of today is much less overt and therefore much less of an obstacle. As a result, the stories of today's black inventors are not much different from the stories of inventors of any other race. No one much notices or cares about the skin color of the Mark Deans and Valerie Baths of our time. In the long run, though, this is not to be mourned but instead to be applauded. The category of "African American inventors" belongs to the past. Today, U.S. society has progressed to the point where only "inventors" exist—creative men and women of whatever race, their skin color far less important than their creations. Without question, that change is all to the good.

Notes

Chapter One: Early Black Inventors

1. James Mitchell, *Answer of the Agent of the Indiana Colonization Society.* Indianapolis: Chapman, 1852, p. 15.

2. Portia P. James, *The Real McCoy: African American Invention and Innovation, 1619–1930.* Washington: Smithsonian Institution, 1989, p. 54.

3. Quoted in James, *The Real McCoy,* p. 53.

4. Quoted in James, *The Real McCoy,* p. 53.

5. Quoted in Sidney Kaplan, *American Studies in Black and White.* University of Massachusetts Press, 1996, p. 232.

6. Quoted in Kaplan, *American Studies in Black and White,* p. 229.

7. Quoted in *The Encyclopedia of Cleveland History,* "Peake, George." http://ech.cwru.edu/ech-cgi/article.pl?id=PG.

8. Quoted in James, *The Real McCoy,* p. 40.

9. *Weekly Wisconsin* (Milwaukee), "Reward of Perseverance," October 13, 1847, p. 2.

10. Quoted in Cowan's Auctions, "Important Ohio Tester Bed, Henry Boyd, Cincinnati." www.cowanauctions.com/upcoming_dates_view_item.asp?ItemId=36486.

11. Michael W. Markowitz and Delores D. Jones-Brown, *The System in Black and White.* Santa Barbara, CA: Greenwood, 2000, p. 141.

Chapter Two: Mechanics and Tinkerers

12. Allan Nevins and Henry Steele Commager, *A Pocket History of the United States.* New York: Pocket Books, 1976, p. 258.

13. Quoted in Mark Aldrich, *Death Rode the Rails: American Railroad Accidents and Safety, 1828–1965.* Baltimore: Johns Hopkins University Press, 2006, p. 104.

14. Quoted in C.R. Gibbs, *Black Inventors from Africa to America.* Silver Spring, MD: Three Dimensional Publications, 1995.

15. *Janesville (WI) Gazette,* "Pullman Company Sued," January 28, 1892, p. 3.

16. Quoted in Bruce Sinclair, ed., *Technology and the African-American Experience.* Cambridge, MA: MIT Press, 2004, p. 58.

17. Quoted in John S. Butler, *Entrepreneurship and Self-Help Among Black Americans.* Albany: State University of New York, 1991, p. 60.

18. *La Crosse* (WI) *Tribune*, "Negro Inventor Versatile," May 30, 1926, p. 6.

19. Quoted in Elaine Nembhard, "Black Inventor Alters Shoe Industry in U.S.," *Ocala* (FL) *Star-Banner*, December 25, 1981, p. 7.

20. Patricia Carter Sluby, *The Inventive Spirit of African Americans: Patented Ingenuity*. Santa Barbara, CA: Greenwood, 2004, p. 40.

21. Quoted in United States Industrial Commission, *Report of the Industrial Commission*, vol. 14, Washington, DC: Government Printing Office, 1901, p. 302.

22. James, *The Real McCoy*, p. 72.

Chapter Three: The Age of Electricity

23. Charles Panati, *Panati's Extraordinary Origins of Everyday Things*. New York: Harper & Row, 1987, p. 136.

24. Charles R. Brooks, "Black Inventor Helped Develop Telephone, Electric Lighting," *The News* (Frederick, MD), February 10, 1971, p. 10.

25. Quoted in Sluby, *The Inventive Spirit of African Americans*, p. 46.

26. Quoted in Kareem Abdul-Jabbar and Alan Steinberg, *Black Profiles in Courage*. New York: Morrow, 1996, p. 210.

27. Quoted in Francis Jehl, *Menlo Park Reminiscences: Part 2*. Dearborn, MI: Edison's Institute, 1939, p. 708.

28. Quoted in Brooks, "Black Inventor Helped Develop Telephone, Electric Lighting," p. 10.

29. Quoted in Rayvon Fouche, *Black Inventors in the Age of Segregation*. Baltimore: Johns Hopkins University Press, 2003, p. 35.

30. Quoted in Fouche, *Black Inventors in the Age of Segregation*, p. 33.

31. Quoted in James, *The Real McCoy*, p. 95.

32. Quoted in Butler, *Entrepreneurship and Self-Help Among Black Americans*, p. 60.

33. Quoted in Teresa Riordan, "Patents," *New York Times*, January 19, 2004, p. C2.

34. S.W. Balch, "Electric Motor Regulation," *Cosmopolitan*, April 1895, p. 761.

Chapter Four: Moving Forward

35. Quoted in Butler, *Entrepreneurship and Self-Help Among Black Americans*, p. 60.

36. Quoted in Ayana D. Byrd and Lori L. Tharps, *Hair Story*. New York: St. Martin's, 2001, p. 34.

37. Quoted in *Waterloo* (IA) *Evening Courier*, "Death of Negress Revives Romance," July 14, 1919, p. 9.

38. Quoted in Madam C.J. Walker: The Official Web Site. www.madamcjwalker.com.

39. *Fort Wayne* (IN) *Journal-Gazette*, "Madam Walker at Mt. Olive Baptist Church," March 12, 1918, p. 11.

40. Quoted in Susan B. Griffith, "Children Raise Funds for Morgan Marker," *Cleveland Call & Post*, July 21, 1994, p. A1.

41. Quoted in *Black Inventor Online Museum*, "Garrett Morgan." www.blackinventor.com/pages/garrett morgan.html.

42. *Sandusky* (OH) *Star Journal*, "Twenty-three Dead in Tunnel Under Lake?" July 25, 1916, p. 1.

43. *Elyria* (OH) *Evening Telegram*, "21 Dead, 9 Hurt in Tunnel Disaster," July 26, 1916, p. 3.

44. Quoted in James, *The Real McCoy*, p. 92.

45. *Black Inventor Online Museum*, "Garrett Morgan." www.blackinventor.com/pages/garrettmorgan.html.

46. Quoted in Gary R. Kremer, *George Washington Carver in His Own Words*. Columbia: University of Missouri Press, 1991, p. 20.

47. Quoted in B.D. Mayberry, *A George Washington Carver Handbook*. Montgomery, AL: New South, 2007, p. 13.

48. Quoted in Kremer, *George Washington Carver in His Own Words*, p. 21.

49. Quoted in Kremer, *George Washington Carver in His Own Words*, p. 20.

50. Quoted in Peggy Robins, "The Gentle Genius," NPS.gov: George Washington Carver National Monument. www.nps.gov/archive/gwca/expanded/gwc_tour_04.htm.

51. Charles Van Doren, ed., *Webster's American Biographies*. Springfield, MA: G. & C. Merriam, 1974, p. 182.

52. *Reno* (NV) *Evening Gazette*, "George Washington Carver," January 7, 1943, p. 4.

Chapter Five: Into the Future

53. Quoted in NPR.org, "Income Gap Between Blacks, Whites Expands," November 13, 2007. www.npr.org/templates/story/story.php?storyId=16257374.

54. Quoted in Dave Kenney, *Minnesota Goes to War*. St. Paul, MN: Minnesota Historical Society, 2005, p. 149.

55. Quoted in Jim Jones, "Thermo King Owes a Lot to Founder's Hot Idea," *Minneapolis Star and Tribune*, June 15, 1987, p. 1M.

56. *New Castle* (PA) *News*, "They Had a Dream," January 24, 1970, p. 3.

57. Quoted in Kenney, *Minnesota Goes to War*, p. 150.

58. *New Castle* (PA) *News*, "Device Guarantees Fresh Vegetables," April 12, 1951, p. 24.

59. *Anderson* (IN) *Herald*, "DePauw to Graduate 6th in Family," May 22, 1970, p. 27.

60. Quoted in DePauw University, "*Sun-Times* Features One-Time 'Chicagoan of the Year,' Percy Lavon Julian '20," February 5, 2007. www.depauw.edu/news/index.asp?id=18849.

61. *News-Journal* (Chicago), "Triton Names Hall for Dr. Percy Julian," April 14, 1976, p. 26.

62. Quoted in Margaret J. Collins, "Patents Granted to Illinois African American Women Inventors Between 1885–2004," Illinois State Library. www.cyberdriveillinois.com/departments/library/what_we_have/pdfs/african-americanwomen-inventors.pdf.

For More Information

Books

Nathan Aaseng, *Black Inventors*. New York: Facts On File, 1997. Each chapter is a short biography of a major inventor. Aaseng is especially good at explaining complicated scientific concepts.

Kareem Abdul-Jabbar and Alan Steinberg, *Black Profiles in Courage*. New York: Morrow, 1996. An interesting account of important African Americans through history, including information on several inventors.

James Michael Brodie, *Created Equal: The Lives and Ideas of Black American Innovators*. New York: Morrow, 1993. Information on a variety of African American inventors, scientists, and others.

A'Lelia Perry Bundles, *On Her Own Ground: The Life and Times of Madam C.J. Walker*. New York: Scribner, 2001. A biography of Walker written by one of her descendants.

Cheryl Harness, *The Ground-Breaking Chance-Taking Life of George Washington Carver and Science and Invention in America*. Washington: National Geographic, 2008. A biographical account of Carver that puts his work in the context of the technological understanding of his time.

Jim Haskins, *Outward Dreams: Black Inventors and Their Inventions*. New York: Bantam, 1992. One of the first young adult books to focus on African American inventors.

Portia P. James, *The Real McCoy: African American Invention and Innovation, 1619–1930*. Washington, DC: Smithsonian Institution, 1989. Well illustrated and informative, this book focuses on black inventors and scientists throughout American history.

Barbara Kramer, *George Washington Carver: Scientist and Inventor*. Berkeley Heights, NJ: Enslow, 2002. Information about George Washington Carver's life and work.

Kristine M. Krapp, *Notable Black American Scientists*. Detroit: Gale Research, 1999. Includes information about Lewis Latimer, Percy Julian, and other scientific figures mentioned in this book.

Beverly Lowry, *Her Dream of Dreams: The Rise and Triumph of Madam C.J. Walker*. New York: Knopf, 2003. A detailed and informative biography of Madam Walker.

Otha Richard Sullivan, *African-American Inventors*. New York: Wiley, 1998. Biographical accounts of important black scientists and inventors. Generally well researched and informative.

Otha Richard Sullivan, *African-American Women Scientists and Inventors*. New York: Wiley, 2001. Biographical information on black women in the sciences. Includes information on Madam Walker and other female inventors.

Glennette Tilley Turner, *Lewis Howard Latimer*. Englewood Cliffs, NJ: Silver Burdett, 1991. A biographical account of Latimer and his electrical inventions.

Web Sites

About George Washington Carver (www.nps.gov/archive/gwca/expand ed/gwc.htm). This Web site of the George Washington Carver National Monument in Missouri gives information about Carver and about the historic site as well. The monument is administered by the National Park Service.

The Garrett A. Morgan Association: Biography (www.fhwa.dot.gov/gama/ gamlife.htm). A Federal Highway Administration site that offers a short biographical sketch of Morgan in the context of his time, focusing mainly on Morgan's traffic signal.

Madam C.J. Walker: The Official Web Site (www.madamcjwalker.com). Provides biographical information, excerpts from Walker's speeches and writings, and links to further points of interest.

NOVA: "Forgotten Genius" (www.pbs .org/wgbh/nova/julian). The companion Web site to the WBGH video about the life of Percy Julian. Includes biographical information and links to other sites.

Videos

Stephen Lyons and Llewellyn M. Smith, *Percy Julian: Forgotten Genius*. Boston: WGBH Boston Video, 2007. A documentary on the life and work of chemist and inventor Percy Julian.

Schlessinger Video Productions, *Madam C.J. Walker, Entrepreneur*, 1992. A video about Madam Walker and the business empire she created.

Index

Picture Credits

Cover: © Bettmann/Corbis

Kike Calvo/VWPics/Visual & Written SL/Alamy, 17

© Roger Coulam/Alamy, 65

© Marvin Dembinsky/Photo Associates/Alamy, 32

© Jeff Greenberg/Alamy, 8

© Image Management/Alamy, 39

© Frans Lemmens/Alamy, 19

© North Wind Picture Archives/Alamy, 13, 31, 54

© Oasis/Photos 12/Alamy, 12

© Peter Worth/Alamy, 78

AP Images, 51, 62, 82, 88

© Bettmann/Corbis, 23, 25, 42, 72, 77, 86

© Library of Congress – digital ve/Science Faction/Historical/Corbis, 70

© Schenectady Museum, Hall of Electrical History Foundation/Corbis, 49

© Corbis, 60

Hulton Archive/Getty Images, 29

The Granger Collection, New York, 59

The Library of Congress, 84

Queens Borough Public Library, 46

Schomberg Center for Research in Black Culture, 67

About the Author

Stephen Currie is a writer and teacher who grew up in Chicago and now lives in New York State's Hudson Valley. He has written and published dozens of books, magazine articles, and educational materials, including a number of volumes in Lucent's *Library of Black History* series. As a boy, he once received an official certificate of merit from the Tinkertoy Company for devising a new way to make a Tinkertoy horse. Beyond that, however, his experience with invention is limited to using and appreciating those created by other people.